CERTIFIED

VERNAL

ALFALFA

60 LBS. NET

Sara Larson Buscaglia

farm & folk
quilt alchemy

A HIGH-COUNTRY GUIDE
TO NATURAL DYEING AND MAKING
HEIRLOOM QUILTS FROM SCRATCH

ABRAMS, NEW YORK

contents

My work as a farmer, artist, and writer takes place on the ancestral land and territory of the Ute people, the traditional stewards of this land since time immemorial, whom the United States government forcibly removed. Since this book is about fibers and natural dyes, I would also like to acknowledge the tragic histories regarding the production of cotton, indigo, cochineal, and logwood that also ensued as the result of European colonization. Hundreds of thousands of Black and Indigenous peoples were subjugated, exploited, enslaved, and forced to produce them as commodities, on which the United States and Europe built empires. To this day Black and Indigenous peoples have not received reparations.

introduction

The moment I was introduced to the ancient art and alchemy of natural colors derived from plants and minerals, I was captivated. Transferring color from plants to fibers seemed like utter magic. That was more than twenty years ago, and after all these years I'm still enamored by the profundity of it, as enamored as I am every spring when I partake in the alchemy of planting seeds that sprout from the earth and become nourishing food that sustains my family.

My husband and I learned organic farming on a whim, by reading books and through a lot of trial and error. In our first years of farming, we dove in headfirst and purchased a flock of sheep, which provided us with their beautiful wool. It was those sheep that inspired me to expand my knowledge of natural dyeing. Every spring I sheared them, and every fall and winter I spun their wool into yarn, naturally dyed it, and knit garments from it to keep us warm. Those

connections—with the homegrown fiber from our beloved sheep friends and with the dye plants' gift of color—were most gratifying. The time it took to create such intentional, cherished, utilitarian items was undoubtedly time well spent.

Many years later, I unexpectedly discovered quilt making and was completely overtaken by the ability to express myself artistically through the medium of fabrics and colors, shapes, and stitches. In the excitement of it all, I briefly overlooked my values regarding consumerism, and began buying designer fabrics and churning out quilts one after another out of pure enthusiasm. Those first quilts I made were fun and a valuable learning experience, but they didn't feel representative of my agrarian lifestyle. Quilts, after all, are an autobiography of sorts. The colors and patterns, fabrics and stitches tell a small piece of the maker's story, and my first quilts didn't feel like they were telling my authentic story. They

Respect to the land, soil, and biodiversity, which nourish us felt rushed and unintentional when compared to those homegrown, handspun, naturally dyed sweaters I loved to make.

The farm itself is a vital teacher in the context of slowness and patience. The many months that pass from the time the first seeds are planted in the spring soil to the final harvest in the fall reveals the true value of food. Eventually I realized that what felt lacking in my quilts was that simple, sacred slowness. I renewed my relationship with the dye plants and took my own advice to support organic agriculture by purchasing organically grown fibers to work with. I took the time to finish these intentional quilts with hand stitches and, in the end, they felt like a more accurate representation of my lifestyle and values.

When I first began naturally dyeing cellulose fabrics, I was expecting the knowledge I gained from dyeing protein-based wool yarns to transfer right over—and it did in some ways, but it wasn't as intuitive as I imagined. Also, I quickly discovered that dye recipes and techniques specific to cellulose fabrics weren't so easy to come by. I had many questions, which led to lots of research and experimentation. It took me several years to figure out how to achieve certain colors and to reproduce specific colors reliably. My intention for this book is to share what I've learned over the years and to answer the biggest questions I had when I first began naturally dyeing cellulose fabrics for quilts. The arts of both natural dyeing and quilt making are so expansive that one could spend a lifetime practicing them and still have plenty to explore. The constant discoveries and evolutions keep it infinitely exciting.

Farming and making things slowly by hand have helped me connect the dots about how certain goods are produced. Being a producer inoculates the mind in that way. Once I began extracting color from plants and transferring it to fibers, I began to think about synthetic dyes and fibers and the magnitude at which they're used. How the waste they create ends up in waterways and has adverse effects on ecosystems. How all life is dependent on these ecosystems directly and indirectly, and the notion that what we do to the earth we do to ourselves, because we're inescapably interconnected.

Farming, quilt making, and anti-consumerism are my main acts of resistance to modern culture. I believe that a good method to protest the egregiously toxic systems currently in place is to collectively stop supporting them. Each time we spend money—or choose not to—we're casting a vote regarding our future and the earth our children will inherit. Collectively ceasing to buy the toxic things we're offered from powerful corporations is a form of peaceful protest. Choosing not to support companies that exploit and endanger workers is a vote cast. Being happy with what we have and ceasing to give in to the "buy more" mentality is revolutionary! Taking time to repair and mend what's broken is too. The acts of planting seeds and taking time to make beautiful, intentional items with our hands offers an opportunity to understand the true value of things. The food I grow, and the sweaters and quilts I make and mend, are acts of resistance. They're equally acts of resilience.

—Sara Buscaglia,
La Plata County, Colorado, 2022

"Just to live here and now—this is the true basis of human life."

—MASANOBU FUKUOKA

how to use
this book

This book is divided into four sections.

The first is an exploration of the alchemy that happens prior to applying natural dye to cellulose fabrics.

The second section is an in-depth study of applying natural dye to fabric yardage, including techniques and recipes to create specific colors.

The third section is dedicated to the art of patchwork—turning beautiful, naturally dyed fabrics into quilts! The projects are presented in a skill-building fashion.

The final section contains tutorials for all of the essential steps in making a quilt from beginning to end. I recommend creating tabs with Post-it notes for easy referencing.

1.
pre-dye alchemy

Fibers:
Cotton
Hemp
Linen
Repurposed Fibers

My Dye Studio:
Dye Apothecary
Project: Dye Apron

Getting Started:
Weigh Your Fabric
Scour Your Fabric
Wet Out Your Fabric
Mordant Your Fabric

My outdoor dye kitchen

Natural dyes require natural fibers, which are categorized as either cellulose- or protein-based. Protein fibers, such as wool and silk, are derived from animals and insects, whereas cellulose fibers, such as linen, hemp, and cotton, are derived from plants. Although beautiful quilts can be made from protein fibers—and I encourage you to make some!—I've decided to focus exclusively on cellulose fabrics for this book.

Besides the incomparable colors, one of the great aspects of dyeing is the freedom in choosing a base fabric, and one thing I look for when shopping for fabric is organic certification. GOTS (Global Organic Textile Standard) certification meets both ecological and social standards, making it a good one to look for. Purchasing organically produced fibers over conventionally produced fibers is a way for consumers to be proactive in resisting GMO agriculture, toxic herbicides, pesticides, and synthetic fertilizers, while simultaneously advocating for living soil and clean waterways, which all life depends upon.

"An organic farmer is the best peacemaker today, because there is more violence, more death, more destruction, more wars, through a violent industrial agricultural system. And to shift away from that into an agriculture of peace is what organic farming is doing."

—VANDANA SHIVA

PFD sashiko thread can be scoured, mordanted and dyed using the same technique and recipes as fabric, but care must be taken to prevent it from becoming tangled.

FIBERS

To determine the thickness of a fabric, manufacturers supply a weight per square yard ratio. For quilting, I look for fabrics roughly in the range of 4½ to 8 ounces per square yard (153 to 271 gsm), although I encourage you to think outside that box and use what feels good to you. It's especially helpful to order samples from suppliers so you can feel the fabric in your hands before committing to purchasing yards of it.

Cotton

Cotton (*Gossypium*) fiber is derived from the hairy seeds of the cotton plant and is native to both the Eastern and Western Hemispheres. The seeds ripen in a pod called a boll. Upon maturity, the hairy fibers are harvested and separated from the seeds, then they're washed, combed, spun, and woven into fabric. To put your cotton clothing or fabric stash into perspective, it takes approximately twenty square feet of a cotton field to yield enough cotton to produce one shirt.

Currently most of the cotton grown in the United States is genetically modified rather than organically grown. This makes it difficult to source domestically grown organic cotton because there's just not much of it, but by collectively purchasing organic cotton fabrics and goods, even if they're imported, we create a demand for it. We have to start somewhere, and creating a demand for it opens a potential market opportunity for domestic conventional cotton farmers to transition to organic growing methods. Refusing to purchase GMO cotton fabric is an active vote against it. Conventional GMO cotton will continue to be the norm as long as consumers support it.

Organic cotton muslin is a great fabric for natural dyes and quilts. It's lightweight yet sturdy and holds its shape when cutting quilt pieces, which is particularly nice for beginner quilters.

Hemp

Hemp (*Cannabis sativa*) is a very strong, durable, long-lasting bast fiber. After harvesting, the stalks must be retted to remove the fiber from the stem. Then the fiber is combed with a tool called a heckle, spun, and woven into cloth. In 1970, the US government banned all cannabis production because of the psychotropic varieties, but thankfully the prohibition era is coming to an end, and cannabis is having a renaissance. Canada and China are currently the largest producers, but US production will become a possibility if consumers create a demand for it. The more people show interest in hemp by purchasing it, the more it can be planted, so buy hemp and hemp-blend fabrics! (And buy organic cotton!) Hemp is a versatile, truly renewable resource that provides not only fiber for textiles and garments but also paper products, building materials, nutritious seeds, cooking oil, biofuel, medicine, and so much more. Pure hemp fabric is available in several different weights, from lightweight to heavy canvas. There are some nice blends available too, and I particularly love the texture of organic cotton-hemp muslin, which dyes beautifully.

Linen

Linen (*Linum usitatissimum*), aka flax, is also a bast fiber and is processed in a similar manner to hemp. Linen is a light yet durable fiber rich in texture that accentuates hand stitches. It can be pretty shifty when cutting, so if you're a beginner you may have a more satisfying experience working with cotton or a cotton-linen blend. When piecing quilts with linen, it's a good idea to set the stitch length on your machine to 1.5 to avoid fraying. When I'm shopping for linen fabric, I look for a weight somewhere around 5½ ounces per square yard (186 gsm), which is often referred to as medium weight. I also look for organic sources with GOTS certification. Linen can be purchased in either its natural color or whitened, both of which are nice to dye. When I'm dyeing dark colors such as black, I often use un-whitened linen as a base fabric. Linen-cotton blends are nice for dyeing and for quilt making. As always, I recommend purchasing samples before purchasing yardage.

Repurposed Fibers

There's a growing trend of artists committed to working with repurposed materials. Used cotton and linen garments, sheets, curtains, and other textiles can be found at home, thrift stores, and flea markets and used in place of new fibers for natural dyeing. If the textile has stains, keep in mind that the stains won't go away when dyed. Incorporating modern or vintage prints with naturally dyed fabrics can yield an unexpected, fun juxtaposition. Working with what we have is very satisfying and can be used as a revolutionary tool to liberate ourselves from the throes of modern consumerism. Some of my favorite quilts are ones with unexpected qualities in which the maker likely used what they had available out of necessity.

I choose not to incorporate synthetic fibers in my quilts because each time they're washed, synthetic fibers shed thousands of microfibers. These microfibers end up in fresh waterways that lead to oceans. There's literally tons upon tons of plastic waste floating around in the ocean, and it's now understood that there's even more microplastic in the ocean than the large pieces that can be seen by the naked eye. I don't want my quilts to contribute to microplastic shedding. Quilts made from natural dyes and fibers can be composted when they reach the end of their lives and returned to the soil to offer fertility for new crops to grow. They do not leave the future with the debacle of how to safely dispose of them. I don't have a solution for what to do with all the fossil fuel fabrics, especially since they're still being produced at such an alarming rate, but I hope we can be more critical of them, and collectively advocate against them when taking into consideration the environmental and health repercussions they pose.

THE DYE STUDIO

Over the years, I've moved my dye studio from the kitchen to various outbuildings on the farm until I finally landed in a permanent studio space in our old barn that we renovated. This new studio consists of a dye studio and sewing studio under one roof and offers me the opportunity to work with natural dyes all year round, If you don't have a studio space, don't let it get you down or deter you. Whatever space you have available is a great place to begin.

You don't need a bunch of fancy things to get started—in fact I encourage you to start out by working with what you have and to take some trips to the thrift store to see what you can find there. Build up your tools slowly and invest in certain items as you can. I've found many of my dye kitchen tools secondhand. My first dye pots were big enamel canning pots from the thrift store that I used for several years, until the enamel began chipping off the inside. They weren't ideal, but they worked until I was able to purchase my beloved heavy-bottomed stainless steel pots. It's taken me many years to dial in and fine-tune my dye studio, yet as I learn and evolve my practices, I add to my inventory accordingly.

Plants and minerals in concentrated forms are potent and unsafe to ingest so it's really important to have separate dye pots, pans, spoons, and other tools from the ones you use to cook food. The following is an inventory of my current dye studio tools and a brief description of what they're used for. If you're just getting started, a large pot, a large spoon, and a scale are the only essentials you need.

A corner of my indoor dye studio in wintertime

DYE APOTHECARY

I stock my dye pantry similarly to how I stock my kitchen pantry, in that there are several main staples I always have on hand. When they get low or run out, I forage, harvest, or order more. I'm always trying new techniques and new dye materials, so the cupboard content is ever evolving. The dyestuffs and supplies that you desire will depend totally upon your palette preference. You may want to make all the colors of the rainbow, or you may prefer a specific curated palette. It's best to store dyestuffs in a dark space, such as a cupboard or box, because they will degrade if stored in direct light. Not every item on this inventory list is required, it's just to give you an idea of the variety I like to keep on hand. For example, you may begin with only one or two tannins rather than purchasing all ten.

My outdoor summer dye kitchen

my dye studio tool inventory

- 1 double-burner gas camp stove (for seasonal outdoor use)
- 1 large electric induction burner (for indoor use)
- Water source (I use a garden hose)
- 4 heavy-bottomed stainless steel dye pots (22-quart/21-L capacity) with lids (for large batches)
- 2 stainless steel pots (10-quart/9-L capacity) with lids (for small batches)
- 1 stainless steel pot (1-quart/1-L capacity) (for extractions)
- 4 plastic buckets (5-gallon/19-L capacity) (for tannins and mordants)
- 2 submersible bucket heaters (I was hesitant to buy these, but recently added them to my tool inventory and they've proven to be very useful. I use one to reheat my indigo vat and the other for reheating tannin and mordant baths.)
- 3 enamel buckets (for rinsing dyed fabrics and for random things like wetting out fabrics, for chalk baths, or heating up water)
- Several large wooden stirring spoons (I have one for scouring, one for mordanting with alum, one for each dye color, one for iron, etc. A couple stainless steel spoons that could be scrubbed clean would be a great option too, but I love my colorful wooden spoons.)
- 1 small metal spoon (for scooping and weighing dyestuffs)
- 1 chef's thermometer (I prefer analog, but digital is fine too)
- 1 stainless steel whisk (for incorporating tannin, mordants, and dyestuffs in water)
- Fine-point permanent markers (for recording fabric weights in selvedges)
- 1 large strainer (to strain dyestuffs off dye baths) and some loosely woven fabric or cheesecloth for lining it
- 1 small fine-mesh strainer (for straining tiny dyestuffs like ground cochineal)
- A few pairs of rubber gloves (for various tasks)
- Dust masks (for wearing when weighing out fine particles)
- 1 triple-beam scale (capable of weighing very small amounts of dyestuffs and mordants and also heavier objects like fabrics)
- 1 small enamel bowl (for weighing dyestuffs)
- Thick terrycloth towels and old wool blankets (to insulate dye pots and hold them at certain temperatures)
- Scissors (for cutting yards of fabrics)
- Clothespins and a cotton clothesline (to dry mordanted and dyed fabrics)
- 1 mortar and pestle (for wetting out indigo or grinding cochineal and other dyestuffs)
- 1 flint striker (for lighting the gas stove)
- Heavy-duty electric herb grinder (for grinding madder root and other homegrown or foraged dyestuffs)
- Stainless steel pads and powder cleanser (for scrubbing dye pots); I use Bon Ami
- pH test strips

my dye apothecary

Scouring Agents
- synthrapol
- soda ash (sodium carbonate)

Tannins
- walnut husks
- myrobalan
- henna
- gallnut
- chestnut
- cutch
- tara
- sumac
- pomegranate
- quebracho

Mordants
- potassium aluminum sulfate
- aluminum acetate
- symplocos
- ferrous sulfate
- calcium carbonate

pH Influencers
- white vinegar
- soda ash (sodium carbonate)
- citric acid
- calcium hydroxide

Dyestuffs
- cutch extract
- cochineal
- Himalayan rhubarb
- indigo powder & fructose
- logwood chips and extract
- finely ground madder root
- osage orange wood chips
- dried weld & weld extract
- black walnut shells or husks
- Hopi Black Dye sunflower seeds
- dried onion skins

MATERIALS

- 1½ or more yards (1.3 or more m) woven fabric (depending on your personal measurements and width of fabric) of linen, hemp, or a hemp-cotton blend. I chose a hemp–organic cotton blend that I dyed with Hopi Black Dye sunflowers at 100% WOF (Formula 8, page 64)
- Matching cotton sewing machine thread

dye apron

This is my favorite style of apron to make and wear when I'm working in the dye studio. It's about as simple as it gets: a rectangle with hemmed edges and straps that cross in the back. This loose-fitting version is best suited for lighter fabrics with drape, such as 4- to 6-ounce (135 to 203 gsm) linen or hemp.

1. Determine your apron width: Measure the fullest part of your chest and add 50% to it. For example, for a bust measurement of 32 inches (82 cm), your apron width would be 48 inches (123 cm), because 32 + 16 = 48 (82 + 41 = 123).

2. Determine your apron length: Measure down from the widest part of your chest to the length you wish your apron to be and add 4 inches (10 cm) for seam allowances. For example, a preferred apron length of 32 inches (82 cm) means the length is 36 inches (92 cm), because 32 + 4 = 36 (82 + 10 = 92).

3. Cut your apron piece to these measurements. Cut two straps, each 6 by 30 inches (15 by 76 cm). (They'll be fitted to you in step 10.) The cutting layout will depend on your fabric size and your personal measurements. When cutting a big piece like this it can be easiest to make a little snip with the scissors through the selvedge and tear the fabric rather than trying to cut in a long straight line.

4. Now fold and pin the top edge, but do not stitch it in place yet. Hem the apron sides first, and then hem the bottom edge: Turn the raw edges to the wrong side (WS) ½ inch (1.3 cm) and press. Fold the edges another 1½ inches (3.8 cm) and press, pinning as you go. Now press and pin the top edge, but do not stitch it in place yet.

5. A longer stitch length looks nice when sewing hems, so set your stitch length to around 3 and edgestitch the hems along the second folded edge.

6. Fold the raw edges of the long sides of the straps ½ inch (1.3 cm) to the WS and press.

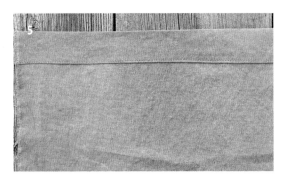

7. Fold the straps in half lengthwise and press, pinning along the folded edges.

8. Topstitch ⅛ inch (3 mm) from the open edges. Repeat to make the second strap.

9. Identify the apron center along the top hem by folding the apron in half. Press the fold to make a crease, then mark 2 inches (5 cm) to the right and left of the center mark. The straps will be placed on the outside of these marks. You may wish to space yours farther apart; hold the apron up to you at this point and mark for your desired strap placement.

10. Determine your strap length: Lay the apron fabric with wrong side up. On one top corner, tuck an end of one strap under the folded hem. Hold the strap in place and fold it up. Press and pin it in place. Repeat for the second strap on the opposite top corner. Cross the left strap over the right and bring it to the outside of the placement mark to the right of center and pin it in place.

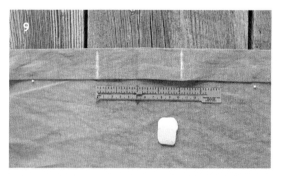

11a. Pin the right strap to the outside of the placement mark to the left of center. Try on the apron, re-pinning the straps at different lengths until you get the apron sitting just how you want it. Before you trim the excess from the straps, be sure to leave an extra 3 inches (7.5 cm) on each strap for seam allowance.

11b. Attach the straps to the front the same way as the back. Edgestitch the hem along the fold, then topstitch ⅛ inch (3 mm) from the top edge.

A Note on Safety

Protect yourself when handling and weighing out natural dyestuffs and mordants. It's not healthy to breathe in dust of any kind, so wear a good dust mask. Plants and minerals are potent. Make it a regular practice to wear gloves when handling all of the various mordant, tannin, and dye baths.

GETTING STARTED

Water is an important factor in natural dye alchemy, and the pH and minerals in your water will influence the colors you can achieve. I suggest working with whatever water you have in its natural state. Get to know your water by testing its pH with pH strips. A pH of 7 is neutral. If your pH is high (basic) or low (acidic), you may eventually want to experiment with adjusting it. The pH can be raised with a small amount of wood ash or soda ash and lowered with vinegar or citric acid.

Rainwater may be a good option if you live in a place where it rains a lot because it's naturally soft, although in some regions contains pollutants (acid rain). Well water and spring water contain various minerals that can, in some situations, make it difficult to achieve clear colors,

Fabrics with the WOF marked on the selvedges

especially if there's iron present. If you are curious, try using 16-in-1 test strips to find out what minerals are present in your water, especially if you're experiencing difficulty in achieving clear colors. Most dyes prefer soft water, but madder root, logwood, and weld have an affinity for the calcium present in hard water, so richer colors may be achieved by adding calcium carbonate to those dye baths.

Weigh Your Fabric

"WOF" is an abbreviation dyers use to express Weight of Fiber. All the natural dye processes require weighing as a first step. To determine how much dyestuff to use for each individual batch, percentages based on the weight of the fiber (WOF) are used. WOF is always taken when the fabric or fiber is dry. You'll need a scale capable of weighing in grams—which is the most frequent unit of measurement used throughout this book and by most dyers—and also pounds (kilograms). I prefer an old triple-beam scale from my kid's homeschooling days because it doesn't require batteries and is capable of accurately weighing very small amounts, which I've had difficulty getting my digital scale to read. A digital scale is admittedly more convenient in its ability to tare weights (zero out a weight) without having to do any extra math. In quilt making, the fabric selvedge is discarded, so I use it as the place to record the WOF and fabric type with a fine-tipped permanent marker. That way I don't have to keep re-weighing the fabric or referring to my notebook throughout the subsequent processes.

Scour Your Fabric

Plant fibers are composed primarily of cellulose, but they also contain small amounts of wax, pectin, and oil that must be removed in a process called scouring. Good scouring is essential in achieving fast, even dye colors that penetrate the fibers. For best results, don't cram too much in the scouring pot. I normally scour 2 yards (1.8 m) of fabric at a time per 5-gallon (19 L) capacity pot. Different cellulose fibers can be scoured together in one pot. All new fabrics need to be scoured before treating them with tannin, mordant, or dye. If you're working with prepared-for-dye (PFD) fabrics, you can skip scouring and simply do a pre-wash in a washing machine. When working with repurposed fabrics, it's helpful to scour to remove any dirt or oils. When dyeing with indigo, you will skip the tannin and mordant baths but you still must scour. It's nice to keep a supply of scoured fabrics on hand.

Scouring Recipe for Cellulose Fibers

- 1% WOF Synthrapol or any mild liquid detergent
- 2% WOF soda ash (sodium carbonate)
- Hot water

1. In a large pot (I use a 5-gallon one), combine the Synthrapol, soda ash, and hot water, stirring to dissolve the Synthrapol and soda ash.

2. Open out and unfold the fabric and carefully submerge it with a large spoon.

3. Set the pot over low heat and let simmer for 1 hour, keeping the fabric submerged. Don't let the water come to a hard boil, or you'll have a dangerous fabric-and-hot-water geyser situation. The water will darken slightly as the fibers release their oils and pectins, especially when scouring cotton.

4. Turn off the heat and let the fabric cool until cool enough to handle.

5. Wring out the fabric, then rinse the soap out either in a sink or in the washing machine on a rinse cycle. Keep the fibers wet if you are proceeding to a tannin bath (see page 32), or hang to dry fully before storing for later use.

Washing soda and synthrapol being weighed out and fabric awaiting scouring

WET OUT YOUR FABRIC

"Wetting out" fabric means to soak it in lukewarm water for at least 20 minutes before entering it into a tannin, mordant, or dye bath. This ensures the most even dye coverage. Fabrics should never be entered into any baths dry. After soaking, wring out the fabric and then shake it open before entering it into any of the baths.

MORDANT YOUR FABRIC

Mordanting is an alchemical process that transforms fibers. Once successfully mordanted, fibers become a permanent foundation for natural colors to bond to. This isn't the most glorious step in the dye process, because you can't see the actual magic that's happening, but without mordant, dye colors would wash off quickly and fade away. When working with cellulose fibers, a two-step mordanting process is required—first tannin, then mordant. There are a handful of dyes that don't absolutely require mordants, but I nearly always follow through with the two-step process to ensure optimal colorfastness results for quilts. Indigo being a substantive dye is an exception to this rule and therefore fabric is not mordanted prior to dyeing with indigo. For the best, most even results, it's important not to crowd tannin and mordant baths. If too much fabric is crammed in these baths, the fabric will have a tie-dye look when dye is applied. One yard (1 m) per 5-gallon (19 L) bucket is my maximum. Make sure the fibers remain completely submerged the entire duration of the steep. If the fabric pokes out of the water for a prolonged period of time, the dye won't attach well to that part. Different fibers take up tannin, mordant, and dyes at different rates, leaving less available for the others, so it's best to separate your fabric by type and treat them in separate mordant baths.

I do not use heavy-metal mordants such as copper, chrome, and tin in my practice. Although there are dye recipes that call for them, they should be avoided, as they are toxic and pose health risks to both the dyer and the environment. For a dyer wishing to avoid metal salts that are mined and refined, symplocos is a renewable mordant to consider.

Soy milk is sometimes referred to as a mordant, but it is technically a binder, because it doesn't facilitate an actual chemical bond between fiber and dye. It will attract dye and hold it like glue but will inevitably wash off, making it an unsuitable application for quilts. Soy milk is better suited for garments and other objects that can easily be dyed again if they fade.

TANNIN

Unlike protein fibers, cellulose fibers don't have the natural ability to readily accept a mordant, but treating them with tannin prior to mordanting increases their ability to do so. When applied properly, tannin may also improve a dye's lightfast qualities. Longer soak times in the tannin and mordant baths often yield optimal colorfastness.

Tannins are categorized as either clear, yellow, or dark. Natural dye suppliers offer a variety to choose from, and you may be able to forage some locally. The different base shades that tannins provide are an amazing tool that can be used as a foundation to build colors on and to broaden

Clear Tannins	Yellow Tannins	Dark Tannins
oak galls	myrobalan	cutch
tara	pomegranate	quebracho
	henna	sumac
		walnuts
		chestnut

palettes. Clear tannins are a preferable option if your goal is to let the color of the natural dye you're working with shine unaltered.

Yellow and dark tannins have a dual purpose as either a pre-mordant or a dye. Yellow tannins impart their color onto fibers, providing a yellow color foundation that can be used as a tool to subtly shift dye colors, or to enhance yellow dyes. Dark tannins provide a tan or brown foundation layer to build dark colors on, or to use as a base for overdyeing. Fabrics that have been treated with tannin will react in an iron bath, shifting the natural tannin colors to various shades of gray, brown, and charcoal depending on the tannin type and the tannin-to-iron ratio. The seemingly endless different tannin base and dye combinations are fun to explore.

Opposite: Ten shades of tannin applied at 10% WOF. From bottom to top: walnut, tara, oak gall, henna, myrobalan, pomegranate, sumac, quebracho, cutch, chestnut

Foraged oak galls are very rich in tannin. Their formation is a strange and magical phenomenon: When a parasitic gall wasp lays her eggs in the tissue of an oak tree, the tree reacts by creating a hard encasement, called a gall, around the eggs, providing the developing larva with food and shelter. When a larva becomes mature it eats its way out of the gall. When foraging for galls, look for ones with a hole, to ensure the wasp larva has made its way out. Galls are a treasure to natural dyers! To make a tannin bath they should be finely ground.

Tannin Bath Recipe

The method of applying tannin is the same regardless of the tannin type. Each color formula recipe includes a suggested type and amount of tannin, but I encourage you to explore beyond my suggestions. There truly is no right or wrong tannin for each dye. All of them will work; it just depends on your color preference. For best results, do not crowd the tannin bath. One yard (1 m) per 5-gallon (19 L) bucket is great. This recipe calls for hot water; hot tap water is sufficient, making it possible to use a plastic bucket instead of heating the water in a dye pot. Tannin will become damaged at high temperatures, making it ineffective in creating a bond for the mordant to attach to, so check the temperature carefully.

- Hot (120°F/50°C) water
- 8 to 20% WOF tannin

1. Fill a 5-gallon (19 L) bucket with hot tap water. The exact amount required will depend on how much fabric you're working with: use enough water for the fabric to remain submerged and not be too crowded in the pot.

2. Add the required tannin to the water, whisking thoroughly until there are no lumps.

3. Submerge the wetted out fabric and let steep for 6 to 24 hours. Longer soaks often yield the best colorfast qualities. Be sure the fabric is completely submerged for the entire duration of the steep for even results.

4. Wearing rubber gloves, wring out the fabric and rinse once very gently with cold water before proceeding to mordanting. It's best

From top left & going clockwise: chestnut, myrobalan, and cutch tannin baths

to move right on to mordanting rather than letting the fabric dry.

Tannin baths can be reused a few times, but should be disposed of if mold begins to grow. To "recharge" a tannin bath, heat it back up to 120°F (50°C) and refresh it with an additional 30% of the called-for amount of tannin.

TANNIN STUDY

Conducting natural dye studies is an invaluable tool for answering questions that arise. Here's a tannin study I did to help me understand the shades that

From bottom right, up along the arch to bottom left: ten shades of tannin, then each of the shades modified with 2% and 4% iron to yield the grays and browns, then dipped once and twice in an indigo vat to yield the blues and greens.

different tannins impart on fibers, and what those shades shift to when modified with iron or indigo. To begin, I made tannin baths with ten different tannins, each at 10% WOF. Then I divided each tannin sample into three equal pieces. I left one piece of each shade unmodified and set them aside. Then I divided each remaining sample in half so I had four pieces of each sample. I modified one sample of each shade with iron at 2% and one at 4% to compare the difference. I discovered that the samples treated at 2% iron yielded grays and at 4% shifted to browns. Then I modified a sample of each tannin shade by dipping it once in my indigo vat, and finally the remaining samples were given

two dips. The one-dip samples yielded teals closer to greens and the two-dip samples yielded teals closer to blues. I love conducting this type of study and learn so much this way. If you come up with a question, conduct a study and be sure to record all your discoveries in your dye journal.

MORDANT

Once cellulose fabric has been transformed through the alchemy of tannin, it has a new ability to readily accept mordants. After a fabric has been successfully mordanted, the result is permanent. The fabric can be kept wet and dyed immediately or hung to dry and stored in a tote to be dyed another time. It's convenient to keep a supply of mordanted fabrics on hand. Label each piece of fabric so you know what type and amount of tannin and mordant were used.

Alum Mordants

"Alum" is an umbrella term for mordants that are aluminum derived. The following are my favorite alum recipes. Always wear a mask when handling alum in its dry form, and wear rubber gloves when handling all alum baths.

Potassium Aluminum Sulfate Recipe

This is my go-to mordant. It's inexpensive and works well in combination with tannin to create very long-lasting colors with good fastness qualities. Potassium aluminum sulfate is refined from bauxite, which is processed first with sulfuric acid and then again with potassium to purify it from iron and other mineral contaminants. Because it has been extensively purified, dyers are able to achieve clear colors with it. Though I use this mordant very often, the more I research aluminum mining and processing and their negative impacts on the environment, the more I am committing to experimenting with plant-based renewable mordants in the future.

- Hot (120°F/50°C) water
- 10 to 20% WOF potassium aluminum sulfate
- 2% soda ash

1. Fill a 5-gallon (19 L) bucket with hot tap water. The exact amount required will depend on how much fabric you're working with: use enough water for the fabric to remain submerged and not be too crowded in the bucket.

2. Stir in the alum, then the soda ash. The soda ash neutralizes the pH, which will cause it to bubble. When the bubbles subside, submerge the fabric and let steep for 6 to 24 hours. Be sure that the fabric is completely submerged at all times to avoid uneven dye results. Wearing rubber gloves, wring out the fabric. Gently rinse once or twice in cold water to remove any unattached alum. Either keep the fabric wet and proceed to dyeing, or hang to dry and store for later use.

Aluminum Acetate Recipe

Aluminum acetate, like potassium aluminum sulfate, is derived from bauxite but is processed with acetic acid as a purifier. Many natural dyers prefer it for cellulose fibers over other mordants because it is said that more saturated colors can be achieved with it. Through my experimenting I haven't noticed enough of a difference to prioritize it. Nonetheless, I encourage you to experiment with it to see what kind of results you're able to achieve with it. Although many natural dye recipes suggest skipping the tannin bath when using aluminum acetate as a mordant, I still prefer to do it because tannin will often enhance a dye's lightfastness qualities.

Note that mordanting with aluminum acetate requires the use of a fixing solution (recipe follows).

- Hot (120°F/50°C) water
- 8 to 15% WOF aluminum acetate

recharging an alum mordant bath

Alum mordant baths can be reused 1 to 3 times or more. If your water is hard, some alum will attach to the minerals in the water and create a grainy texture or dark color. When this happens, dispose of the bath and begin a new one. Although I have hard water, I still reuse my alum baths 2 to 3 times each before evaporating them. If I'm going for a strong color, such as madder red, I'll always begin with a fresh alum bath rather than a recycled one.

To recharge, heat the bath to 120°F (50°C) either on the stovetop or with a submersible bucket heater. Add 30% of the required amount of mordant called for in your recipe.

1. Fill a 5-gallon (19 L) bucket with hot tap water. The exact amount of water required will depend on how much fabric you're working with: use enough water for the fabric to remain submerged and not be too crowded in the bucket.

2. Add hot water to a small bowl, then stir in the aluminum acetate to form a thin paste. Add the paste to the vessel and whisk until no lumps remain.

3. Submerge the fabric and let steep for 6 to 24 hours. Be sure that the fabric is completely submerged at all times to avoid uneven dye results. Prepare the fixing solution (recipe follows).

4. Wearing rubber gloves, transfer the fabric to the fixing solution, submerge, and let steep for 5 to 10 minutes. Wring out the fabric and rinse once gently with cool water. Either keep the fabric wet and proceed to dyeing, or hang to dry and store for later use.

Fixing Solution Ratio
Always wear a mask when weighing out powders.

- 30 g calcium carbonate (chalk) to 1 gallon (4.5 L) hot (120°F/50°C) tap water

In a 5-gallon (19 L) bucket, stir the calcium carbonate into the water. Use enough water for the fabric to remain submerged and not be too crowded in the bucket.

Symplocos Mordant

Symplocos trees, native to eastern Asia, are hyperaccumulators of aluminum, which is stored in the leaves. Dried fallen leaves contain the highest amounts of aluminum. There are more than two hundred species of symplocos, a few of which can be found growing throughout the northeastern United States. If symplocos can be found in your region, you can gather the fallen leaves and grind them to a coarse consistency in a blender (one used only for dyeing). If you can't forage it locally, many dye suppliers offer a Fair Trade Certified source. Symplocos is rather new to me, but the prospect of a nontoxic, renewable mordant that doesn't have to be mined is exciting. Symplocos will impart a light yellow tint to the fabric.

Symplocos Mordant Recipe

- 50% WOF symplocos

1. Fill a large dye pot with water, heat to a near boil, and add the symplocos. Cover and keep at a gentle simmer for 1 hour. Symplocos gives off a very strong, sweet smell, which I find to be pleasant at first, but it quickly can become overwhelming. Since it has to simmer for so long, I recommend working outdoors if possible.

2. Strain off the bath. Submerge the wetted out fabric and let steep for 24 hours.

3. Wearing rubber gloves, gently rinse the fibers once in cold water. Either keep the fabric wet and proceed to dyeing, or hang to dry and store for later use.

Iron Mordant or Modifier

I use iron, also referred to as ferrous, as a mordant prior to dyeing black and other dark colors but more commonly as a color modifier to shift dye colors to a darker, "saddened" hue. When modifying yellows and other lighter shades, begin with 1% WOF. A little iron goes a long way, but if you need to add more, lift the fabric out of the pot, quickly add more, give it a good stir, and then return the fabric to the pot. For darker color shifts, ferrous can be used at up to 4%. When dyeing fabric black, up to 5% WOF can be used, but don't exceed 5% or the bath may become unsafe to handle and dispose of.

When iron is being used as a color modifier, the fabric will remain in the bath for a short period. When using iron as a mordant, the fabric will require more time in the bath. It's tricky to

Cotton fabric fresh out of a symplocos mordant bath

achieve even results in an iron bath; the key truly is to keep the fibers constantly moving. An iron bath can often improve the fastness quality of certain dyes, like logwood, but prolonged soak times will damage fibers, so don't mordant longer than 30 minutes. Because iron can significantly influence a dyes color, I often prefer to begin with a fresh iron bath rather than to take my chances with reusing them. It's best to designate one pot exclusively as the iron bath pot because it's difficult to clean iron from it, and the smallest, tiniest bit will sadden your colors. Make sure to clean all your work surfaces thoroughly after handling and weighing out iron, or you'll inevitably notice little iron-speck stains on your fabrics. Once iron modified or mordanted fabric is thoroughly rinsed, washed, and dried, it will not contaminate other fabrics, making it totally okay to put it in a quilt with white and other light colors. Always wear rubber gloves when working with ferrous in all stages, from weighing it out to rinsing the dyed fabric, and as always, wear a mask when working with powders.

Iron Bath Recipe

- 1 to 5% WOF ferrous sulfate

1. Put on rubber gloves and keep them on throughout this entire process. Fill a large dye pot with water and heat it to 140°F (60°C). Add the ferrous and stir well.

2. Submerge the wetted out fabric in the iron bath and stir constantly, keeping the fabric moving—the entire time the fabric is in the iron bath, it must be moving, or you will not achieve even results!

3. Check the color and remove the fabric just before you've achieved your desired shade, because the fabric may darken slightly after you remove it. Lift the fabric out of the bath and rinse it once or twice in cold water, then wring it out and hang to dry.

TANNIN, MORDANT, AND DYE BATH DISPOSAL

I've scoured dye books for information on proper disposal of dye baths and have found such conflicting information! I think what it comes down to—at least this is true for me—is that most natural dyers are artisans and not chemists. There's still so much to learn about natural dye safety, and discoveries are constantly being made. If you're on a municipal water system, all of the mordant and dye recipes can be disposed down the drain after straining off the dyestuffs. The following is how I currently dispose of my various baths, but as the years go on and new discoveries are made this may become bad advice, so please do your part to keep your ears perked for evolving information.

I'm on a septic system, which relies on a fragile microbial balance to properly function, so I don't dump any baths down my drain. I check the pH of all baths before dumping them and neutralize with wood ash (to reduce acidity) or vinegar (to combat a base mixture) accordingly. I dump scouring baths in my gravel driveway. I dump tannin baths in the wood-chip section of our back driveway. I keep a couple of 50-gallon (190 L) drums in the corner of my greenhouse—one to evaporate spent alum baths and one for spent iron baths. Evaporation happens quickly in my climate, but may not be an option in less-arid areas. I compost most dye baths and spent dyestuffs, with the exception of logwood and black walnut: logwood contains hematein, which is moderately toxic, and walnut trees release a natural herbicide called jugalone that I don't want to introduce to the compost, so I dump these spent dye baths in our gravel driveway. I burn strained logwood and black walnut bits in our outdoor fire pit. Strained symplocos baths are dumped on the lawn. I compost organic fructose indigo vats (page 60) after neutralizing the pH. To neutralize, I stir vigorously to bring oxygen into the vat and add vinegar if needed.

2.
color alchemy

All of the color recipes!

"From this fine art you find the secret of imitating what is most beautiful and charming in nature and you can truly say that it is the spirit which brings to life everything it touches." – GIOCHIN BURANI, 1794

Dyestuffs, minerals, and natural fibers are gifts from the natural world, born through the sacred alchemy of soil, seeds, photosynthesis, sunlight, moonlight, and rain. Over the ages, humans have tended to dye plants through the acts of foraging, cultivation, harvest, and selective seed saving, and the dyestuffs have reciprocated by providing us with their gifts of color. When transferred to fibers, these colors are a tangible embodiment of nature's perfect imperfections. The subtle yet profound variations make them more alluring than the perfectly uniform results of synthetically dyed fibers. When the alchemy is good, natural dyes yield lasting rich colors that have the potential to grow even more beautiful over time.

Humankind has been dyeing fibers since time immemorial. For thousands of years, all dye colors were derived from natural sources—until 1856, when the first synthetic dye was mistakenly discovered by eighteen-year-old William Henry Perkin as he attempted to synthesize the anti-malarial drug quinine. Synthetic dyes were inexpensive to produce and comparatively easy to apply. Quite suddenly the art and alchemy of natural dye was largely abandoned and buried in the dust of the industrial revolution. Modern natural dyers are taking part in a revolutionary act by reviving the sacred reciprocal relationship between humans, natural dyestuffs, and fibers, and that's so exciting because these seemingly small acts are the very things that shift the collective mind and inspire cultural reset.

The world of natural dye alchemy is so extensive that it would be impossible to master it all in one lifetime. Before synthetic dyes were introduced, natural dye houses were specific to one color so the artisan dyers were typically masters of only one color. As modern natural dyers we have the opportunity to explore the alchemy of many colors. The constant stream of new discoveries keeps it infinitely exciting and inspiring. Currently there's a growing trend of artists working with naturally derived color in various mediums. There are many historical recipes and dyestuffs that are tried and true and also new plants, recipes, and natural dye extracts to explore.

I occasionally work with extracts, but my preferred method is to extract the dye myself from raw materials. The fragrant alchemical experience of standing over a bubbling pot of leaves, bark, flowers, roots, and occasionally bugs is a valuable step in my process because it connects me to the raw source. I love actually witnessing the color emerging from the dyestuff—it just never gets old! When purchasing fibers and dyestuffs, do some research to ensure they're foraged or farmed responsibly and ethically. The natural dye revolution is not a good one if our fellow humankind, plant friends, and resources are being exploited. If you're foraging for dyestuffs, be conscious to

Depth of shade gradation from onion skins

take only what you need, which may be none at all if there's not an abundance. As a further step, we can replenish natural supplies by spreading native seeds in areas that have been over-foraged.

DEPTH OF SHADE

Depth of shade, DOS, is a value that refers to how pale or deep a color is on fiber. For example, madder root at 100% WOF will often produce a true red and at 8% WOF a coral pink. It's invaluable to gain an understanding of what depth of shade is achieved at different WOF percentages for each dye plant. Keep in mind there's no right or wrong WOF percentage for any dye plant. The ratio is based entirely on your shade preference. If, for example, you dyed fabric to a color that was more saturated than you were hoping for, simply decrease the WOF next time to get a lighter shade. If you achieved a pastel shade when you were hoping for a more saturated shade, you'll want to increase the WOF. Keeping a detailed dye journal with samples is the most valuable tool for remembering what shades you're able to achieve at different WOF percentages with your personal alchemy.

Samples of an original dye bath on the right and a diluted exhaust bath on the left

Right: A gradation dyed with yellow onion skins

For quilt making, my desire is most often to create a gradation (ombré) consisting of many DOS out of each dye bath, but there are times that I need to create several yards that are the *same* DOS. In that case, instead of making a gradation I make a couple dye baths of the same WOF percentage, enter the fabrics into the dye baths at the same time, and remove them at the same time so the fabrics are all dyed the same DOS.

When making a gradation of color, the first dye bath yields a strong, saturated color, and each subsequent bath, which dyers refer to as exhaust baths, provides a less-saturated DOS. Colors born of the same pot are like family—related yet individual and unique. I find them to be most inspiring for quilt making. Once the gradation is created, I often modify some of the pieces with either iron or indigo and sometimes both to further expand the palette. A positive attribute of the ombré exhaust bath method is that very little precious

dye goes to waste. For an ombré dye session it's necessary to have several yards of scoured and mordanted fabric prepared. I normally dye two ½-yard (50 cm) pieces of fabric at a time, so I have one to keep as it is and one to modify. Please note that when weighing out dyestuffs to set up an ombré bath, the WOF percentage required for the color formula you're following applies only to the first piece (or pieces) going into the first dye bath. All of the following baths are exhaust baths in which the WOF is irrelevant. Achieving a shade gradation isn't always as simple as entering subsequent pieces into the exhaust baths and achieving lighter shades with each bath. Some exhaust baths will remain very strong, producing shades nearly as saturated as the first. In this case you'll need to pour off some of the dye bath—save it in jars for another day—and dilute what's left with more water. This diluted bath will yield a lighter shade. Fabrics must be kept in the dye pot and held at the proper temperature (see each recipe) for a full hour or more to facilitate a permanent colorfast dye-to-fabric bond, which is why you can't just remove the fabric after a shorter amount of time. Often—but not always!—the most saturated and evenly dyed colors will be achieved by steeping fabrics in the dyepot overnight at room temperature.

ACHIEVING EVEN COLORS

Even dyeing is something that comes with practice and patience, and of all fibers, cellulose-based fabric yardage is the most difficult to dye evenly. Here's a checklist to help you achieve evenness:

- Scour thoroughly to ensure the mordants and dye can penetrate the fibers.
- Don't overcrowd the tannin and mordant baths.
- Be sure the fabric is completely submerged for the entire steep time in the tannin, mordant, and dye baths.
- Rinse once with cold water after the mordant bath to remove any excess unattached alum.
- When working with aluminum acetate, be sure to use a fixing solution after mordanting and then rinse once in cold water to remove any unattached alum.
- Add the fabric to the dye bath when it reaches about 120°F (50°C), then slowly bring the bath up to temperature. Adding cold fabrics to a very hot dye bath can cause unevenness and streaking.
- Keep the fabric in the dye pot for at least 1 hour, holding at the specified temperature. Pull the fabric out after 1 hour and look at it. If it's even and you're happy with the DOS, remove it. Steep overnight for potential deeper color and improved evenness.

COLOR FORMULAS

The alchemy of transforming undyed fibers to colorful ones is the most exciting part of the natural dye process, because you can actually see it happen, unlike the invisible alchemy of mordanting. Please understand that you will not achieve the exact shades that I do—there are so many variables with natural dyes. You yourself will not likely be able to produce the very exact same shade every single time. I have a deep appreciation for this lack of total control and find it to be a wonderful aspect of this work. Each color

dye bag

Most of the time I let the dyestuff float around the dye pot, but sometimes better results are achieved by containing it in a dye bag. When the dyestuff touches the fabric, it can leave saturated marks (for example when working with chopped madder root I suggest using a dye bag.) Any loosely woven fabric like gauze or cheesecloth can be used to make one. Use yarn or string to tie the bag closed.

that comes out of the dye pot is a unique treasure that may, yet may not, be reproducible. And here I go again reiterating that experimenting and keeping a dye journal full of extensive notes will be your best tool along the way.

All fabrics must be scoured as a first step. All fabrics, with the exception of those that will be dyed with indigo, must also be pre-treated with tannin and mordant, the amounts of which are provided in each color formula (see pages 44–79). Read through the entire instructions for each formula before beginning.

Madder Root (*Rubia tinctorum*)

Madder root is an ancient dye plant native to the Middle East, the Mediterranean, and Northern Africa. Traces of madder-dyed linen were discovered in King Tutankhamen's tomb in Egypt and it has also been identified in Norse burial grounds. It produces classic, very colorfast shades of gorgeous reds and is the dyestuff historically used to make the color turkey red. I achieve true madder reds by making a dye bath of finely ground cured roots. An electric Chinese herbal medicine grinder does a beautiful job grinding dried madder root to a fine powder. The grinder is an investment but is great for grinding other dyestuffs you might grow and forage, such as oak galls, walnut hulls, symplocos, weld, and dried pomegranate skins. If you don't grow your own madder root, you can purchase it finely ground from a dye supplier. The main red dye constituent in madder is alizarin, which is sensitive to heat, so grind just twenty seconds or so at a time, letting the blender cool in between to avoid damaging it. If the alizarin becomes damaged from high temperatures in the blender or dye bath, the red potential may be lost, and in its place the remaining dye constituents will produce brick reds and browns.

Cultivation: *Rubia tinctorum* is a hardy rhizomatic perennial that grows well in many climates. It grows so well, in fact, that it has the potential to become an invasive weed. To grow your own, plant madder seeds in starter trays around six weeks before your average last frost date, then transplant the seedlings to the garden once the danger of frost has passed, spacing them about 18 inches (45 cm) apart. It takes at least three full years for the roots to become large enough to harvest, making it a cherished dyestuff. The longer you wait to harvest it, the thicker the roots will be. Plant a new generation of seedlings every spring to get on a yearly harvest cycle.

Harvesting madder root in August

Dried madder root freshly ground to a fine powder

Madder stems have cruel, spiky hairs that will scratch your skin and cause a painful rash, so always wear long sleeves and gloves when handling the plant tops or when weeding around them. To harvest, cut back the plant tops and dig the roots with a shovel or digging fork. Lay them out on a screen or basket and spray the soil off with a hose. Cut the roots into small pieces with pruning shears and spread them out to thoroughly dry out of direct sunlight. The roots must be dried completely to develop the best dye potential; giving them several weeks to cure before making a dye bath is ideal. Leave some plants to continue growing, because late in the summer they'll produce little star flowers, which become berries. When the berries begin to dry, collect some before the birds eat them all, for these are the seeds you'll plant next spring. Make sure the seeds are dried thoroughly before storing them, or they will become moldy.

FORMULA 1: MADDER ROOT RED

When working with finely ground madder, I never achieve a very exciting ombré gradation (see page 42) and therefore compost the dye bath after the first red shade is achieved. Interestingly, though, when working with chopped madder root (see page 49), I am able to achieve a nice gradation.

Pre-mordant with tannin at 15%, steeping 24 hours. Different tannins will subtly alter the final shade of red that you achieve. Myrobalan

yields red-orange, chestnut tannin yields a rich dark red, and oak galls a clear madder red. Mordant with potassium aluminum sulfate at 15% WOF, aluminum acetate at 10% or symplocos at 50%, steeping for 24 hours. Repeating the mordant process may yield richer shades. Weigh out dry cured madder root pieces at 125% WOF and grind it to a fine powder. Fill the dye pot with enough water to submerge the fabric. If you have soft water, whisk 1 teaspoon calcium carbonate per gallon of water into your dye pot. Add the finely ground madder to the dye bath and stir well. Heat the bath to 100°F (40°C), then add the

fabric, completely submerging it. Over low heat slowly bring the bath up to 170°F (75°C). Hold the dye bath at temperature for 1 hour, being careful not to exceed 180°F (80°C), stirring often and keeping the fibers submerged. Remove from the heat. To achieve a richer shade, let the fabric steep overnight (8 to 12 hours). Rinse and dry the fabric according to the directions on page 80, and dispose of the dye bath according to the recommendations on page 37.

Note: One scour is almost always sufficient, but when I'm trying to achieve strong reds with madder, I'll often scour and mordant twice.

Dyeing with Chopped Madder Root: If you're unable to source finely ground madder root, and do not have the tools to grind your own fully, you can substitute chopped roots. Dyeing with coarse madder requires making extractions. For a true red with chopped roots, you'll need to increase the WOF to 150 to 200%.

Soak the chopped roots overnight in warm water, then blend them coarsely with the soaking water, with a kitchen blender dedicated to dyestuffs. Pour the blended roots into a dye pot, and add some more water. Heat to 170°F (75°C), then remove from the heat, put a lid on the pot, and wrap it in towels or blankets to keep the heat in. Steep for 1 hour, then strain the dye liquid into a dye pot. Repeat with the same roots twice more, adding the liquid to the same dye pot. Contain the roots in a dye bag and add them to the dye bath. Follow the same dye instructions as for dyeing with finely ground madder. Steep overnight for richer, more even shades.

FORMULA 2: MADDER PINK

Note: Recycled tannin and mordant baths are fine for madder pink.

Treat fabric with clear or yellow tannin at 8% WOF, steeping for 6 to 24 hours. Then mordant with potassium aluminum sulfate at 10% WOF, aluminum acetate at 8% WOF, or symplocos at 50% WOF, steeping for 6 to 24 hours. Weigh out finely ground madder root at 10% WOF. Fill the dye pot with enough water to submerge the fabric. Add the ground madder to the dye pot and stir well. Heat the bath to 120°F (50°C), then add the fabric, completely submerging it. Slowly bring the bath up to 160°F (70°C). Hold the bath at temperature for 1 hour, stirring occasionally and keeping the fibers submerged. Rinse and dry the fabric according to the directions on page 80, and dispose of the dye bath according to the recommendations on page 37.

Cochineal (*Dactylopius coccus*)

Cochineal is a parasitic scale insect native to South America and Mexico that colonizes nopal, also known as prickly pear cacti. Indigenous peoples of Mexico have been selectively breeding the insects for their red pigment, which the female insects contain, for thousands of years.

Cochineal can be purchased online directly from family farms or from reputable dye suppliers who purchase directly from producers. It's a pH-sensitive dye, so the color you achieve will depend on your water. It's a very concentrated dye—a little bit goes a long way. At 10% WOF it will yield a saturated fuchsia shade, and at 3% a bubble gum pink. It can be mixed with other dyestuffs in combination dye pots or overdyed to achieve secondary and tertiary colors. Iron will shift cochineal pinks to smoky purple-gray shades, and indigo will shift it to violet and lilac purples.

FORMULA 3: COCHINEAL PINK & PURPLE

Be sure to pre-treat a lot of fabric, as a beautiful gradation can be achieved with cochineal. It's difficult to exhaust a cochineal dye bath!

For clear colors, use clear tannin at 8% WOF, steeping for 24 hours. Mordant with potassium aluminum sulfate at 15% WOF, aluminum acetate at 10% WOF, or symplocos at 50% WOF, steeping for 24 hours. Grind the dried bugs to a fine powder with a mortar and pestle. Weigh this out to 8% WOF of the first piece of fabric being dyed. Boil the cochineal in a small amount of water for 10 minutes. Strain the dye liquid into the dye pot through a fine-mesh strainer. Repeat this extraction process at least three more times for a

> ### note
>
> For smoky purple grays, modify the pink fabrics in a ferrous bath of 1 to 2% WOF. I especially love the purple shades achieved by modifying cochineal pinks with a dip or two in the indigo vat.

total of four extractions using the same ground cochineal, or until the bugs cease to release much color. Compost the spent bugs. Top off the dye pot with enough water to submerge your fabric. Heat the bath to 120°F (50°C), then add the fabric, completely submerging it. Slowly bring the bath up to 170°F (75°C). Hold the bath at temperature for 1 hour, stirring often and keeping the fibers submerged. Rinse and dry the fabric according to the directions on page 80. Use the exhaust baths to create a gradation, holding each piece in the dye bath for one hour at 170°F (75°C). To achieve lighter shades with each exhaust bath, it may be necessary to pour off some of the dye bath and dilute what's left by adding water. When done dyeing, dispose of the dye bath according to the recommendations on page 37.

Top row: cochineal ombré + Bottom row: 1–2 the ombré shades modified with indigo, 3–5 iron, 6–8 iron + indigo

note

I don't use WOF to dye with onion skins; rather, I use up my year's supply of skins in one concentrated bath.

For greens, dip the dyed fabrics 1 to 3 times in the indigo vat, depending on the shade you desire and the strength of both your onion dye and indigo vat. To "sadden" the shades as shown in the photo, modify with iron, at 1 to 2% WOF (weight of first piece of fabric), entering each piece one at a time and using the exhaust ferrous bath for each subsequent ombré exhaust bath piece you wish to modify, adding more ferrous to the bath only if necessary.

Onion Skins (*Allium cepa*)

One thing about being a modern natural dyer is that we get excited about *all* the colors. We stand over every dye pot oohing and ahhing because we're able to see the beauty in the colors for what they are, rather than for what society deems they're worth. The color that onion skins give has never been a color of desire that kings and queens and clergy grew rich from. It's not derived from the precious heartwood of a tree that takes over a decade to grow or from a rare, endangered mollusk. It comes from one of the most common staple kitchen foods that's easy to grow. To me, it's often the colors I grow that are most special because of the connection I have with them from seed to sprout to harvest to cloth and everything

in between. Many food waste dyes are not very colorfast, but I've found yellow onion skins to be an exception. Red onion skins can be used for dye, but the golden shades you see here came from yellow skins. When modified with indigo and iron, the yellow onion skin palette expands into a groovy 1970s time capsule.

Cultivation: The best way to grow onions is to start them by seed (not sets) indoors in late winter and then transplant them to the garden in early spring, spacing the plants about 6 inches (15 cm) apart. You do not need to wait for the last frost to pass before planting them, because they acclimate best in cold weather. Onions should be harvested in early fall before the hard frost comes and then cured in a dry place. I lay mine out on tarps on the greenhouse floor and rotate them every so often. When the tops have dried, remove them and store the onions in a cool, dark place. As you eat through your stash, save the papery skins in a paper bag and look forward to the summer day you will dye with them!

FORMULA 4: YELLOW ONION SKINS

Have plenty of pre-treated fiber on hand, as this is a concentrated dye bath that works very well for the ombré method. You may need to pour off some of the dye bath and top it off with water to achieve lighter shades with the exhaust baths.

Choose your tannin based on your desired final shades: Dark tannin will produce ochre shades, yellow tannins will enhance the golden yellow onion skin color, and clear tannin produces unaltered onion skin shades. Use your tannin of

Top row: onion ombré + Bottom row: first 6 modified with iron; last 6 modified with indigo

choice at 8% WOF, steeping for 8 to 24 hours. Mordant with potassium aluminum sulfate at 10% WOF, aluminum acetate at 8% WOF, or symplocos at 50% WOF, steeping for 24 hours. Loosely fill a large dye pot half to three-quarters full with onion skins and top with water. The more skins, the stronger the color. Bring the bath to a low simmer and hold it there for one hour. Pour the dye through a strainer and into another dye pot and compost the spent skins. Top off the dye pot with enough water to submerge your fabric.

Heat the bath to 120°F (50°C), then add the fabric, completely submerging it, and bring the bath up to 160°F (70°C). Hold the dye bath at temperature for 1 hour, stirring occasionally and keeping the fibers submerged. Rinse and dry the fabric according to the directions on page 80. Keep the dye bath at 160°F (70°C). Work your way through the exhaust baths to create a gradation, holding each piece at 160°F (70°C) for 1 hour. When done dyeing, dispose of the dye bath according to the recommendations on page 37.

Weld (*Reseda luteola*)

Weld, also known as dyer's rocket, is native to Europe and Western Asia and has been used historically as a dye since prehistoric times to produce very lively colorfast shades of yellow. The dye is derived from the leaves, stems, and flowers. It yields strong, sunshiny yellows at 35% WOF and pastel yellows at 10%. When modified with iron, weld yellows will shift to army and khaki greens, and when overdyed with indigo, beautiful greens from Kelly greens to seafoam shades can be achieved. Many secondary colors can be produced by overdyeing weld yellows or by creating combination dye pots such as weld and madder for oranges or weld and a touch of logwood for greens. Weld develops best in hard water, so adding a bit of calcium carbonate will often brighten the yellow.

Cultivation: Weld is a fairly simple-to-grow biennial. The seeds are tiny, and I always have the best luck starting tiny seeds in seedling starter trays. About six to eight weeks after the danger of frost has passed, carefully transplant the seedlings to the garden. The first year the plants make a

rosette of leaves, and the second year the rosettes tower up into a flowering stalk, providing a lot more mass to work with. Fortunately, there always seem to be a few plants that will flower the first year. Harvest the plants when about half of the flowers on the stalk are blooming and hang them upside down to dry out of direct sunlight. Once dry, shake the seeds out into a paper bag and save them for next year's planting. Use clippers to chop the plants into one-inch pieces and store in jars.

FORMULA 5: WELD YELLOW

Treat with clear or yellow tannin at 10% WOF, steeping 24 hours. Dark tannins, such as chestnut, will produce ochres with this recipe. The natural unwhitened color of linen fabric will yield yellow-greens out of the first dye bath. Mordant with aluminum acetate at 8% WOF, potassium aluminum sulfate at 15% WOF, or symplocos at 50% WOF, steeping 24 hours.

Dye the fabric: For a strong, radiant primary yellow, weigh out the chopped plant matter to 35% WOF of the first piece of fabric being dyed. Fill the dye pot with enough water to submerge the fabric. Add the weld to the dye pot and stir well. Heat the bath to 120°F (50°C), then whisk in 1 teaspoon calcium carbonate per gallon of water. Add the fabric to the dye bath, completely submerging it. Slowly bring the bath up to 160°F (70°C). Hold the dye bath at temperature for 1 hour, being careful not to exceed 160°F (70°C), stirring often, and keeping the fibers submerged. Rinse and dry the fabric according to the directions on page 80. Keep the dye bath at 160°F (70°C). Use the exhaust bath to create a gradation, holding each

Top row: weld ombré + Bottom row: 1–5 modified with
1% iron and 6–11 dipped in indigo between 1 and
3 times

subsequent piece of fabric at 160°F (70°C) for 1
hour. When done dyeing, dispose of the dye bath
according to the recommendations on page 37.
Note: To modify with iron for shades of tan and
brown as shown in the photo, begin with a bath
of 1% WOF, increasing to 2% if necessary. For
true greens, dip 1 to 3 times in the indigo vat,
depending on the strength of your vat.

note

To modify with iron to achieve tans and browns as shown in the photo, use 1 to 2% WOF. For a range of greens, dip 1 to 3 times in an indigo vat, depending on the strength of your vat and your desired shade.

To achieve the olive green for the Ode to Summer Quilt on page 101, pre-treat the fabric in a gall tannin bath of 10% WOF, then mordant with 10% WOF potassium aluminum sulfate. Dye each piece of fabric in a dye bath of 30% WOF osage so they are all the same DOS, then shift them to olive green in an iron bath of 1% WOF.

Osage Orange (*Maclura pomifera*)

Osage orange is a tree native to Texas and other surrounding states, but it now grows in many areas east of the Mississippi. Traditionally it's used by the people of the Osage Nation to make bows. The dye is derived from the heartwood of the tree and produces deep, saturated, colorfast yellows. At 35% WOF, osage yields deep golden yellows, and at 10%, pastels. Once an osage gradation is achieved, the varying yellow hues can be modified with iron to achieve a range of shades from rich golden browns to khaki-tans. When dipped in an indigo vat, a range of greens from primary leafy greens down to pistachio shades can be achieved. Beautiful secondary shades are created by combining osage with other dyes in combination dye pots or by overdyeing.

Top row: osage ombré + Bottom row: 1–5 modified with indigo, 6–8 indigo + iron, 9–10 iron 2%

FORMULA 6: OSAGE GOLD

Have plenty of pre-treated fiber on hand, as osage works very well for the ombré method.

Treat with clear, yellow, or dark tannin at 10% WOF, steeping for 24 hours (dark tannin will produce ochres). The natural unwhitened color of linen fabric will yield darker golds and near ochres. (Among all the fibers I use, linen is the only one that comes in a natural dark color. Dyes will look darker on unbleached linen—just as using darker shades of tannin will also influence dye colors.) Mordant with potassium aluminum sulfate at 15% WOF, aluminum acetate at 10% WOF, or symplocos at 50% WOF, steeping 10 to 24 hours. Weigh out the wood chips to 35% WOF of the first piece of fabric being dyed. Place the chips in a dye pot, cover them with hot tap water, and steep 8 to 24 hours. After steeping, bring the chips to a low simmer for 30 minutes. Top off the dye pot with enough water to submerge your fabric. Bring the bath up to 120 to 140°F (50 to 60°C), then add the fabric, completely submerging it. Slowly bring the bath up to 180°F (80°C) and hold it at temperature for 1 hour, stirring often and keeping the fibers submerged. Rinse and dry the fabric according to the directions on page 80. Keep the dye bath at 180°F (80°C). Use the exhaust baths to dye subsequent pieces of fabric, holding each piece at 180°F (80°C) for 1 hour. To achieve lighter shades with subsequent dye baths, it may be necessary to pour off some of the dye bath and dilute what's left by adding water. When done dyeing, dispose of the dye bath according to the recommendations on page 37.

Indigo (*Indigofera tinctoria*)

Indigo-bearing plants are native to both the Eastern and Western Hemispheres, and there have been samples of ancient indigo-dyed textiles discovered all over the world.

Several plant species produce indigo in their leaves. The most common species that are available from dye stockists are *Indigofera tinctoria* and *Persicaria tinctoria*. Indigo is a rather simple plant to grow, but I won't go over it here because the process of extracting the pigment is extensive, and there are many books and resources that share the process better than I can. I encourage you to look into it! I purchase natural pigment either directly from producers or from natural-dye stockists who have established relationships with farmers. Indigo is a substantive vat dye, meaning fabrics do not need to be treated with tannin or mordant prior to dyeing, rather the colorfastness and permanent bond is facilitated through an alchemy that happens in the vat where insoluble indigo pigment is transformed to its soluble state. Depending on the vat type, alchemy, number of dips, and amount of pigment in the vat, indigo provides shades of blue that range from the palest sky blues to deep midnight blues that are nearly black.

There are many different ways to set up an indigo vat, all of which rely on three main ingredients: natural indigo powder, a reducing agent, and a base. Vat alchemy may seem complicated, but it's pretty straightforward if you don't overthink it. Since indigo powder is naturally insoluble, a reducing agent is needed to transform it to a water-soluble state. For this to take place, the reducing agent requires an alkaline environment, so the pH must be raised to 11 to 12.

The organic 1-2-3 fructose vat, first introduced by Michel Garcia, is a great place to begin. It's simple enough to set up and maintain, nontoxic, and great for dyeing cellulose fabrics, and it can be composted in the end. Every summer I set up a 30-gallon (114 L) fructose vat or two for dyeing fabric yardage, and I keep at least one of the vats going throughout the year. If you're new to indigo alchemy, begin with a small 5-gallon (19 L) vat to gain an understanding and confidence in the alchemy before committing to a large vat. To successfully dye fabric yardage, a large vat is ideal, but you can dye fat-quarter-sized pieces in this vat.

The deepest, most even and colorfast indigo blue shades are best achieved by layering color on top of color via subsequent dips in the vat rather than by achieving a dark blue shade in one dip. A fresh vat set to a medium strength will yield strong dark blues in about five dips. After many weeks or months of dyeing from and maintaining that vat, there will be less indigo present and the blue shades will become lighter. Just as it's ideal to achieve dark shades via several dips, the most even and colorfast light blue shades are achieved by dipping several times in an elder vat that contains less pigment. One dip in a newer vat may give you that light shade you desire, but a single dip won't provide even or colorfast results. Maintaining both a newer, medium-strength vat and an older, weaker vat will provide you with both light and dark shades. If you don't want to wait for those light blue shades or you simply prefer the light blue shades, you can set up a weaker indigo vat by adding less pigment, but I've found that the best light blue shades come from an older vat.

To maintain an indigo vat, it will need to be warmed frequently. A stainless steel pot that can be put on the stovetop is a great vessel. A plastic bucket also works if you have a submersible bucket heater, which is what I use to heat my plastic drum vats.

Calcium hydroxide (lime) which is used as a base in this recipe, will settle to the bottom of the vat, and it's important to keep your fabric from steeping in that sediment. Place a barrier such as an overturned basket at the bottom of the vat to keep the fabric out of the sediment. If the lime gets stirred up and embedded into the fabric, it may prevent the indigo from bonding with the fabric. You'll notice this effect when you're rinsing and the color continuously bleeds off. This color bleed, which dyers refer to as crocking, will also happen if the vat becomes excessively alkaline. Use accurate test strips or a pH wand to determine the pH of your vat.

The fructose vat 1-2-3 ratio is: 1 part natural (non-synthetic) indigo powder, 2 parts lime (calcium hydroxide), and 3 parts fructose. Depending on the strength of vat you prefer, you can use anywhere between 2 to 10 grams of indigo per quart of water; simply adjust the 1-2-3 ratio accordingly. These instructions are for a 5-gallon (19 L) vat set at a medium strength of 7 grams of indigo per quart of water. To set up a larger or smaller vat, simply increase or decrease the amounts of everything accordingly.

Setting up a 5-gallon indigo vat. Stirring the ingredients in a circular vortex motion

FORMULA 7:
FRUCTOSE INDIGO VAT

For a medium-dark vat of 7 grams indigo per quart of water. Note: Fabric to be dyed in an indigo vat does not require pre-treating with tannin or mordant, but does require scouring.

- 18 quarts (17 L) water
- 126 g organic indigo powder
- 252 g lime (calcium hydroxide)
- 378 g fructose

Have a 5-gallon (19 L) bucket or large stockpot ready to become the vat. Set aside. Heat the water

Light, medium, and darker shades of indigo, depending on vat strength and amount of dips

in a large pot to a near boil, then remove from heat. Meanwhile, use a funnel to place the indigo powder in a small plastic bottle from the recycler with a dozen or so marbles. If you don't have a small funnel you can make one with a piece of paper. A 16-ounce water bottle is an appropriate size. Fill the bottle about one-third of the way with hot tap water and screw the lid tight. Shake vigorously for about ten minutes to hydrate the indigo. Pour 4 quarts of the heated water into the vat and stir in the wetted-out indigo. In a separate pot or bucket, combine 4 quarts of the heated water with the fructose and stir to dissolve the fructose. Add it to the vat. While wearing a mask, in a separate pot or bucket, combine 4 quarts of the heated water with the lime and whisk to dissolve the lime. Add it to the vat. Gently pour the remaining 6 quarts of the heated water to the vat and stir the vat with a long-handled spoon or broom handle in a circular motion for about 3 minutes, until all ingredients are incorporated. Be careful not to create bubbles, which would bring oxygen into the vat, compromising it. Put a lid on the vat and let it sit 24 hours in a warm place—to maintain temperature, wrap the vat in towels and blankets. This process is known as reducing. After it has reduced for 24 hours, there should be a coppery-looking film on the surface of the water and a "flower" of bubbles and indigo pigment. If there is no flower, don't worry—the color of the liquid is more important than the presence of a flower. The liquid below the surface should be a clear amber or yellowish green shade. If it's not clear and more of a thick, murky blue, then your indigo has likely not become soluble and you'll need to do some troubleshooting.

TROUBLESHOOTING INDIGO

Oftentimes simply heating a vat, stirring it, and giving it time to settle will get it going, so begin there.

If heat and stirring don't get it going, check the pH. For cellulose fibers it should be 11 to 12. If it's below that, add a little calcium hydroxide and stir in a circular vortex motion. Heat the vat to 100 to 120°F (40 to 50°C) and let it settle for a couple of hours.

If the pH is correct and the indigo is still not reduced (the liquid is murky blue instead of clear green or amber), heat the vat to 100 to 120°F (40 to 50°C), add a handful of fructose, and stir again. Check the liquid after a couple of hours to see if it's shifting from murky blue to clear amber or yellow-green reduced indigo.

5. Keep the fabric submerged. It's important to work very gently because an excess of oxygen compromises vat alchemy. Move the fabric around gently during the 10-minute dip, making sure to keep it fully submerged and that it's opened up and not folded onto itself.

6. After 10 minutes, gently lift the fabric out of the vat, keeping it close to the surface and being careful not to create many bubbles.

7. Gently wring out the fabric as close to the surface as possible. When working with smaller pieces, you can wring them out while they're submerged to create fewer bubbles. With more yardage, just be slow and gentle and stay close to the surface.

8. Submerge the fabric into the bucket of cold water, opening it up to make full contact with the water. It will be green or greenish yellow when removed from the vat, but as it oxidizes in the water it becomes blue. Stir the fabric around in the bucket and go ahead and create lots of bubbles.

9. After 30 seconds or so, wring out the fabric and hang it out of direct sunlight to finish oxidizing. Let each piece oxidize about 15 minutes before doing another dip.

10. Repeat steps 4 through 8; a minimum of 3 dips is necessary to produce the best colorfast shades.

11. When you've reached your desired shade via subsequent dips, hang the fabric to dry out of direct sunlight. Indigo dyed fabric must be pH neutralized after dyeing. See page 63 for proper rinsing instructions.

Indigo-Dyeing Cellulose Fabrics

1. Soak the fabric in warm water with ⅛ teaspoon washing soda (soda ash) for 20 minutes, then wring it out. Open out the fabric before entering it in the vat.

2. If your vat has a flower, scoop it out and put it aside in a bowl for safe keeping.

3. Place a bucket of cold water next to the vat.

4. Submerge the fabric into the vat slowly and gently to create as few bubbles as possible.

12. When your dyeing is done for the day, heat the vat up to 120°F (50°C) and check the pH. If it's below 11, stir in a small amount of calcium hydroxide to bring the pH back up to 12. Feed your vat with a small handful of fructose and give it a good stir in a circular vortex motion, creating a flower at the surface. If you removed an indigo flower before dyeing, replace it now. Put a lid on the vat and wrap it in towels to keep it warm until the next day.

note

If you take a break from dyeing for a while, follow the directions in step 12 to revive your vat. A vat can be revived even if it's been idle for several months, as long as it's not moldy, in which case you should compost it.

indigo pH-neutralizing rinse

Since the pH of an indigo vat is very high, fabric that's been dyed in it will have a chalky, alkaline feeling that's unpleasant. If the pH is not neutralized, the alkalinity will damage the fabric and the color will crock. Begin the process by following the normal rinsing instructions on page 80. Once the fabric is rinsed, do a 30-minute diluted vinegar soak. Use roughly 1 tablespoon of white vinegar per gallon (3.7 L) warm water. You will notice the blue brighten as the fabric neutralizes.

Indigo Overdye

Many secondary colors can be produced with indigo, and there are different ways to do this. One method is to dye the fabric with indigo first, then apply tannin, mordant, and dye to that fabric. Another, less orthodox, method is to take fabric that has already been dyed (using the tannin, mordant, and dyeing process) and overdye it with indigo. Since my go-to method of dyeing is to create an ombré gradation, I usually prefer to create my gradation first, and then overdye some of the fabrics with indigo.

No matter the order you choose, the best way to understand what secondary shades you can achieve is to experiment a whole bunch. See what happens when you overdye a strong osage yellow in a strong indigo vat. Then dip that piece a second time, and maybe a third, to see what happens. Overdye a strong yellow in a weaker vat to see what happens, and so on and so forth. Weld yellows will yield different greens than osage yellows when overdyed with indigo. It's infinitely fun to explore this. If you do the mordanting and dyeing first, be sure to rinse the fabrics well before introducing them to your indigo vat so you don't get color bleed in your vat. Keep samples and notes in your dye journal so you can come back to them next time. If you're feeling wary, tear off a sample strip of fabric to do a test run in the vat before committing to dyeing the entire piece.

Indigo is such a fun and amazing tool to broaden a palette! Fabrics that've been dyed and then shifted with iron can also be overdyed with indigo, to even further broaden the palette. So many possibilities! Note: All fabrics that have been dyed or overdyed with indigo will need to be pH neutralized (see box at left).

Hopi Black Dye Sunflowers (*Helianthus annuus macrocarpus*)

This beautiful sunflower variety was bred by the Hopi people who traditionally use it to dye cotton and basketry fibers. The anthocyanin dye constituent in the seeds is pH sensitive, so the color you achieve may vary according to your water. For me, Hopi sunflowers yield shades of tan and brown, but I've seen other dyers achieve purples, maroons, and grays. I've achieved near blacks when pre-mordanting with iron.

Cultivation: To grow your own sunflowers, plant the seeds directly into the garden once the danger of frost has passed, spacing them at least 1 foot (30.5 cm) apart. The plants grow to be massive in height—6 to 10 feet (1.8 to 3 m) tall—becoming a magical sunflower forest! Sunflowers are a welcome sight to the bird population. As soon as you notice the sunflowers attracting birds, you'll need to net the heads with whatever you have, like cheesecloth, burlap, or gauze fabric and string to protect them from being eaten before you can harvest them. Let the seeds finish ripening on the stalk until the flower heads are heavy and the seeds are black and fully formed, then harvest the heads and bring them in to dry before the first frost comes. Sunflower stems aren't as brutal as madder plant tops, but they do have spiky hairs that can get embedded in your arms and cause irritation. It's best to wear long sleeves when harvesting them. I like to leave a stem of about 1 foot and hang the sunflower heads in bundles of six or so upside down from the barn rafters. The seeds are easier to remove from the flower heads when they're dry. To do this I wear thick leather gloves and rub the seeds out of the flower heads. A lot of chaff will be in the seeds, so winnow it off. A simple way to winnow seeds is to pour them several times from one bucket to another in front of a blowing fan. To prevent mold, make sure the seeds are fully dry before storing them in a jar. A dye bath can be made from either fresh seeds or dry.

FORMULA 8: HOPI SUNFLOWER

Use any tannin at 10% WOF, steeping 12 to 24 hours. Mordant with potassium aluminum sulfate at 10% WOF, aluminum acetate at 8% WOF, or symplocos at 50% WOF, steeping 12 to 24 hours. Remove the sunflower seeds from the flower head and weigh out 100 to 300% WOF—the more you use the stronger the shades will be. I don't always weigh out the seeds; I work with what I have. When working with fresh sunflowers, I'm not meticulous about removing the seeds from the flower head. The seeds are not easy to remove from a freshly harvested flower head, and it's okay to get some pieces of the flower head in the dye bath. Place the seeds in the dye pot, cover them in nearly boiling water, and let steep a few hours. Add enough water to the dye pot to cover the seeds, and bring them up to a simmer for about 1 hour, then strain out the seeds. Top off the dye pot with enough water to submerge your fabric

Top row: Hopi Sunflower ombré + bottom piece was mordanted with iron

Heat the bath to 120°F (50°C), then add the fabric, completely submerging it, and slowly bring the bath up to 180°F (80°C). Hold the dye bath at temperature for 1 hour, stirring occasionally and keeping the fibers submerged. Check on the fabric after 1 hour: If you're happy with the shade you've achieved, rinse and dry the fabric according to the directions on page 80. For a potential darker shade, leave the fabric to steep for several more hours—even up to overnight. Use the exhaust baths to create an ombré gradation, holding each piece at 180°F (80°C) for 1 hour.

When done dyeing, dispose of the dye bath according to the recommendations on page 37.

Cutch (*Acacia catechu*)

Cutch is an extract powder derived from the wood of the acacia catechu tree. It is native to India and the arid regions of Pakistan and Burma, where it has been used as a natural dye since ancient times. It yields dusty pinks at 10% WOF and rich, earthy red-browns at 35% WOF. A cutch dye bath has a lovely pungent, sweet, rich molasses kind of smell and is super difficult to exhaust, making it a perfect candidate for the ombré method. When modified with iron, the colors will shift to a range of rich soil and chocolate browns. Although not pictured, beautiful shades can be created when overdyed with indigo.

FORMULA 9: CUTCH BROWN OR PINK

Have plenty of pre-treated fiber on hand, as cutch works very well for the ombré method. Use tannin at 8% WOF and steep for 8 to 24 hours. Darker tannins will yield darker shades. Mordant with potassium aluminum sulfate at 10% WOF, aluminum acetate at 8% WOF, or symplocos at 50% WOF and steep 10 to 24 hours. Weigh out the cutch extract at 35% WOF of the first piece of fabric being dyed. Fill the dye pot with enough water to submerge the fabric. Heat the water to 120°F (50°C), then add the cutch extract, whisking

Top row: cutch ombré + Bottom row: modified with 2% iron

well until no lumps remain. Add the fabric to the dye bath, completely submerging it and slowly bring the bath up to 180°F (80°C). Hold the dye bath at temperature for 1 hour, stirring often and keeping the fibers submerged. Check the color: If you would like it darker, leave it to steep in the bath for longer, until it reaches the color you want. For rich cutch shades, I often leave fabrics steeping in the dye bath for 24 to as much as 48 hours. Rinse and dry the fabric according to the directions on page 80. To create a gradation, work your way through the exhaust baths holding each piece at 180°F (80°C) for 1 hour. Cutch baths are difficult to exhaust, so to achieve lighter shades with subsequent dye baths, it may be necessary to pour off some of the dye bath and dilute what's left by adding water. When done dyeing, dispose of the dye bath according to the recommendations on page 37.

Quebracho (*Schinopsis quebracho-colorado*)
Derived from the hardwood of evergreen trees native to South America, quebracho is a dual-purpose dye plant that can be used as either a dark tannin or a beautiful dye. The colors are similar to what cutch (page 67) yields, and the dye bath even smells similar and is equally difficult to exhaust. Despite its yielding similar shades to what cutch and Himalayan rhubarb (page 68) yield, I love using the colors side by side, as I did in the Jackrabbit Quilt (page 107). Such subtle differences are so inspiring to me.

FORMULA 10: QUEBRACHO

Have plenty of pre-treated fiber on hand, as quebracho works well for the ombré method.

Use any tannin at 10% WOF, steeping for 8 to 24 hours. Mordant with potassium aluminum sulfate at 10% WOF, aluminum acetate at 8% WOF, or symplocos at 50% WOF, steeping for 12 to 24 hours. Weigh out the quebracho at 15% WOF of the first piece of fabric being dyed. Fill the dye pot with enough water to submerge the fabric. Add the quebracho to the dye pot and stir well. Heat the bath to 140°F (60°C), then add the fabric, completely submerging it and slowly bring the bath up to 170°F (75°C). Hold the dye bath at temperature for 1 hour, stirring occasionally and

> **note**
>
> The warm quebracho pink will shift to a lavender gray in an iron bath of 2%.

keeping the fibers submerged. Check on the fabric after 1 hour: If you're happy with the shade you've achieved, rinse and dry the fabric according to the directions on page 60. If you'd like the fabric to be darker, let the fabric steep up to 24 hours. To create a gradation, work your way through the exhaust baths, holding each piece at 170°F (75°C) for 1 hour. To achieve lighter shades with subsequent dye baths, it may be necessary to pour off some of the dye bath and dilute what's left by adding water. When done dyeing, dispose of the dye bath according to the recommendations on page 37.

Himalayan Rhubarb (*Rheum emodi*)
This dye is derived from the roots of a rhubarb species that grows in the Himalayan mountain region and Tibet. It is not the same rhubarb species we make pies from here in North America. Himalayan rhubarb is pH sensitive and will yield shades between gold and reddish-browns depending on what's present in your water. My water yields earthy brown shades very similar to what I achieve with cutch (page 67) and quebracho. If your water's alchemy yields golden yellows, you can shift them with indigo to achieve a range of green shades.

FORMULA 11: HIMALAYAN RHUBARB

Have plenty of pre-treated fabric on hand, as Himalayan rhubarb works well for the ombré method.

Use a clear tannin at 10% WOF, and steep for 10 to 24 hours. Mordant with potassium aluminum sulfate at 10% WOF, and steep for 10 to 24 hours. Weigh out the Himalayan rhubarb at 30% WOF of the first piece of fabric being dyed. Fill the dye pot with enough water to submerge the fabric. Add the Himalayan rhubarb to the dye pot and stir well. Heat the bath to 120°F (50°C), then add the fabric, completely submerging it, and slowly bring the bath up to 170°F (75°C). Hold the dye bath at temperature for 1 hour, stirring occasionally and keeping the fibers submerged. Check on the fabric after 1 hour: If you're happy with the shade you've achieved, rinse and dry the fabric according to the directions on page 80. If you'd like the fabric to be darker, leave it to steep for as long as 24 hours. Work your way through the exhaust baths to create a gradation. For each subsequent piece of fabric, hold the bath at 170°F (75°C) for 1 hour. To achieve lighter shades with subsequent dye baths, it may be necessary to pour off some of the dye bath and dilute what's left by adding water. When done dyeing, dispose of the dye bath according to the recommendations on page 37.

Shades from quebracho formula 10 on top + Himalayan Rhubarb on bottom

69

Black walnut husk

note

An iron bath at 2 to 4% WOF will shift the browns to grays and near blacks. To make black, pre-treat the fabric with a gall tannin bath at 10% WOF and steep 12 to 24 hours. Then mordant with iron at 5% for 30 minutes and enter the fabric directly into a strong black walnut dye bath, holding the temperature at 180°F (82°C) for 1 hour.

Black Walnut (*Juglans nigra*)

Black walnut is a large deciduous tree species native to eastern North America. The trees are prolific producers of edible nuts that are encased in an outer hull, which is the source of dye. If you are able to forage them locally, select the freshly fallen nuts that are still green. If you can't forage them locally, dye suppliers sell coarsely ground dried husks. Black walnut trees are protective of their space. Their roots secrete a chemical called juglone, which is a natural herbicide that prohibits certain plants from growing. Jugalone also happens to be the dye colorant found in the husks, and it can be irritating to some people's skin, so always remember to wear gloves when working with this dye bath. Dried black walnuts will yield shades between chocolate browns at 50% WOF and beiges at 10% WOF. Fresh will yield these shades at less than half these percentages. Black can be achieved with iron as a mordant.

FORMULA 12: BLACK WALNUT BROWNS

Have plenty of pre-treated fiber on hand to dye a black walnut husk gradation.

Pre-treat fabric in a tannin bath of 8% WOF, steeping for 8 to 24 hours. Mordant with potassium aluminum sulfate at 10% WOF, aluminum acetate at 8% WOF, or symplocos at 50% WOF, steeping for 10 to 24 hours. Weigh out the dried black walnut husks at 50% WOF of the first piece of fabric being dyed, or 20% if you're using fresh husks. If you have an abundance of fresh husks, and you want to dye a deep saturated color, don't feel like you need to stick to 20% WOF. Go ahead and make a strong dye bath with what you have. Fill the dye pot with enough water to cover them. Add the husks to the dye pot and boil them for 1 hour, then strain them off and dispose of them. I burn them in the fire pit to keep the jugalone out of my compost. Top off the dye bath with enough liquid to submerge your fabric and bring the temperature up to 120°F (50°C). Add the fabric, completely submerging it, and slowly bring the bath up to 180°F (80°C). Hold the dye bath at temperature for 1 hour, stirring often and keeping the fibers submerged. Often a darker shade can be achieved if you keep the bath at temperature for another hour or two, stirring often. Turn off the heat and let the fabric steep in the dye pot up to 24 hours, keeping the fibers submerged. Rinse and dry the fabric according to the directions on page 80. Work your way through the exhaust baths to create a gradation of shades, holding each subsequent piece at 180°F (80°C) for 1 hour or longer. When done dyeing, dispose of the dye bath according to the recommendations on page 37.

Top row: black walnut ombré + piece on bottom modified with iron at 2%

Neutral shades created with various exhaust baths + a piece of undyed fabric on the bottom to compare depth of shades

Neutral Colors

A variety of light neutral colors are amazing to incorporate into a quilt. Use diluted exhaust baths of walnuts, cutch, Hopi sunflowers, osage, left-over tannin baths, etc. to very subtly dye fabrics. The exhaust baths should be very diluted, so the fabrics can be left in the dye pot for at least 45 minutes and still be dyed very lightly in shade.

FORMULA 13: EXHAUST BATH NEUTRALS

Make a tannin bath with gall nuts at 8% WOF, steeping for 6 to 24 hours. Mordant with potassium aluminum sulfate at 8% WOF, steeping for 6 to 24 hours. Heat the diluted exhaust dye bath to 120°F (50°C), then add the fabric, completely submerging it. Slowly bring the bath up to 160°F (70°C) and hold the dye bath at temperature for 45 minutes to 1 hour, stirring often and keeping the fibers submerged. Rinse and dry the fabric according to the directions on page 80. When done dyeing, dispose of the dye bath according to the recommendations on page 37.

Logwood (*Haematoxylon campechianum*)

This rich purple dye is derived from the heartwood of the logwood tree, which is native to Mexico. Logwood yields deep shades of eggplant purple at 25% WOF and smoky lavenders at 10% WOF. I rarely use it as a standalone dye, because it doesn't have great lightfast qualities, but iron improves its lightfastness and shifts the dye toward shades of purple-grays; black can be achieved with an iron mordant prior to dyeing. When dipped in the indigo vat, the darkest logwood purples will shift to dark navy blues, and the lighter purple shades will shift to Egyptian blues in a weak indigo vat. I especially like the shades achieved when mixing logwood with cochineal and then overdyeing with indigo, as shared in Formula 18 (page 77).

FORMULA 14: LOGWOOD PURPLES AND NAVY BLUES

For deep purples, make a tannin bath with quebracho or sumac at 10% WOF, steeping for 10 to 24 hours. Mordant with potassium aluminum sulfate at 12% WOF, aluminum acetate at 8% WOF, or symplocos at 50% WOF, steeping for 12 to 24 hours. Weigh out the logwood at 25% WOF. Place the wood chips in a dye pot, top the dye pot off with hot tap water, and steep for 3 to 12 hours. Heat the dye bath to 120°F (50°C), then add the fabric, completely submerging it, and slowly bring the bath up to 160°F (70°C). Hold the dye bath at temperature for 1 hour, stirring often and keeping the fibers submerged. Rinse and dry the fabric according to the directions on page 80. Work your way through the exhaust baths if you wish to create a gradation, holding subsequent pieces of fabric at 160°F (70°C) for 1 hour. When done dyeing, dispose of the dye bath according to the recommendations on page 37.

Top row: a light and dark shade of logwood + Bottom row: 1–2 modified with indigo, 3 iron at 2%

Top row: ombré black shades + Bottom: a saturated black dyed linen

Logwood Black

Naturally dyed black fabric is gorgeous! It has a complex, smoky, organic look and incredible depth, which is achieved through the process of layering tannin, mordant, and dye. Hand stitches on naturally dyed black fabric are incomparable. Despite how long it took me to figure out how to achieve a true black, it's an easy and pretty quick color to make. Achieving even color is most reliant upon successful iron mordanting. The exhaust tannin, iron, and dye baths will yield an ombré of grays.

FORMULA 15: BLACK + GRAY

Make a tannin bath with gall tannin at 15% WOF, steeping for 12 to 24 hours. Weigh out logwood at 25% WOF. Place the wood chips in a dye pot, top the dye pot off with hot tap water, and steep for 8 to 24 hours. Heat the dye bath to 130°F (55°C) and adjust the heat to hold the temperature steady. Meanwhile, set up an iron bath of 5% WOF. Heat the iron bath to 130 to 140°F (55 to 60°C), then add the fabric, completely submerging it. Stir constantly for 25 minutes. Remove the fabric, wring it out, and enter it directly into the dye bath without rinsing. Slowly bring the dye bath up to 180°F (80°C). Hold the dye bath at temperature for 1 hour, stirring often and keeping the fibers submerged.

Remove the fabric, wring it out, and rinse it in a bucket of cold water to remove the excess dye. Hang the fabric to dry, then wait a couple of days before doing the final rinsing according to the directions on page 80.

note

Using the exhaust dye baths will yield lighter orange sherbet shades.

Combination Color Formulas

The recipes shared on pages 46–74 have come from individual dyestuffs, but sometimes you may wish to create a color that a single dye plant can't provide. Cue combination dye pots!

It usually takes a good amount of experimenting to achieve the very color you have in mind, but developing new color recipes and fine-tuning them is fun stuff. If you have a specific color goal, it sometimes helps to look up how to create that color with paint. Creating it with dye won't be the same, but it's helpful to get a general idea of the color makeup. When I experiment with mixing new colors, I set up tiny dye baths, dye small swatches, and keep track of WOF ratios. Taking detailed notes is imperative here. When I finally get a color just right on a swatch, I'll test it on a big piece of fabric and fine-tune the recipe further if needed. Here are a couple formulas I've come up with. I hope they'll get you inspired to try some color mixing of your own!

FORMULA 16: TANGERINE

This formula is a combination of osage and madder.

Make a tannin bath with gall or yellow tannin at 8% WOF, steeping for 12 to 24 hours. Mordant with potassium aluminum sulfate at 12% WOF, steeping for 24 hours. Weigh out the osage wood

First dye bath on the left and the exhaust bath on the right

chips to 25% WOF. Weigh out finely ground madder root at 8% WOF. Fill the dye pot with enough hot tap water to submerge the fabric and add the osage and madder. Heat the bath up to 140°F (60°C), then add 1 teaspoon calcium carbonate and whisk well to combine. Submerge the fabric in the dye bath and slowly bring the bath up to 170°F (75°C). Hold the dye bath at temperature for 1 hour, stirring often and keeping the fibers submerged. Rinse and dry the fabric according to the directions on page 80. Work your way through the exhaust baths for an ombré gradation. For each subsequent piece, hold the bath at 170°F (75°C) for one hour. To achieve noticeably lighter shades with subsequent dye baths, it may be necessary to pour off some of the dye bath and dilute what's left by adding water. When done dyeing, dispose of the dye bath according to the recommendations on page 37.

Ochre shades on the left + ochre with increased chestnut on the right

FORMULA 17: OCHRE

Make a tannin bath with chestnut extract at 8% WOF, steeping for 12 to 24 hours. Mordant with potassium aluminum sulfate at 10% WOF, steeping for 12 to 24 hours. As explained in the tannin section, dark tannins can be used as either a tannin or a dye, and in the case of this recipe both. Chestnut extract can be purchased either in a liquid form or a powdered form. When testing this recipe I used powder.

Weigh out the osage wood chips to 30% WOF. Weigh out chestnut extract at 10% WOF. Fill the dye pot with enough water to submerge the fabric. Add the osage and chestnut extract to the dye pot and stir well. Heat the bath to 120°F (50°C), then add the fabric, completely submerging it and slowly bring the bath up to 180°F (80°C). Hold the dye bath at temperature for 1 hour, stirring occasionally and keeping the fibers submerged. Rinse and dry the fabric according to the directions on page 80. To continue dyeing using the exhaust bath for an ombré gradation, hold each subsequent piece at 180°F (80°C) for 1 hour. To achieve lighter shades with subsequent dye baths, it may be necessary to pour off some of the dye bath and dilute what's left by adding water. When done dyeing, dispose of the dye bath according to the recommendations on page 37.

FORMULA 18: PURPLE

Combining logwood and cochineal will yield a range of colorfast, happy purple shades depending on the WOF percentage used for both dye-stuffs. Have fun playing with and tweaking the WOF of both dyes to discover the purples that can be achieved. This recipe is stronger in cochineal than logwood and will yield an amethyst purple. By reversing the order and making the logwood stronger than the cochineal, you will achieve a deep plum purple. Create an ombré gradation by working through the exhaust baths. The first dye bath will yield that amethyst shade; I've found the logwood to be stronger in the exhaust bath, yielding that ripe plum shade. Combination dyes can be interesting like that! Once the gradation is created, select some pieces to overdye in your indigo vat to achieve a complex range of blues, from Prussian to Egyptian blues.

Make a tannin bath with gall tannin extract at 10% WOF, steeping for 12 to 24 hours. Mordant with potassium aluminum sulfate at 10% WOF, steeping for 24 hours. Grind dried cochineal bugs to a fine powder with a mortar and pestle. Weigh this out to 10% WOF. Boil the cochineal in a small amount of water for 10 minutes. Strain the dye liquid into the dye pot through a fine-mesh strainer. Repeat this process at least three more times for a total of at least four extractions using the same ground cochineal, or until the bugs cease to release much color. Compost the ground bugs. Top off the dye pot with enough water to submerge your fabric. Weigh out the logwood chips at 5% WOF and add it to the dye pot. Heat the bath to 120°F (50°C), then add the fabric, completely submerging it, and slowly bring the bath up to 180°F (80°C). Hold the dye bath at temperature for 1 hour, stirring occasionally and keeping the fibers submerged. Rinse and dry the fabric according to the directions on page 80. To continue dyeing using the exhaust bath for an ombré gradation, hold each subsequent piece at 180°F (80°C) for 1 hour. To achieve lighter shades with subsequent dye baths, it may be necessary to pour off some of the dye bath and dilute what's left by adding water before adding the next piece of fabric. When done dyeing, dispose of the dye bath according to the recommendations on page 37.

A gradation of purple achieved by working through the exhaust baths

Different strengths of myrobalan and indigo to create light and dark shades

in a stronger vat. In this formula I suggest using myrobalan as a light yellow base layer, because it imparts its color without the aid of a mordant. Alternatively, the lightest shades of yellow from an osage or weld gradation could be used to create this color.

Make a tannin bath with myrobalan at 20% WOF, steeping for 24 hours. Rinse the fabric well until the color stops bleeding off. Then dip the fabric for about 3 minutes in a weak indigo vat that's yielding sky blue shades. Once the fabric has oxidized, look at it to check the evenness. A second, shorter dip will improve evenness and colorfastness. The exhaust myrobalan bath can be reused to dye subsequent pieces yellow, and the bath can be refreshed as explained in the tannin bath recipe on page 32.

FORMULA 19: SAGEBRUSH

This is one of my favorite colors, and it shows up in so much of my work. The depth of shade you achieve is based on the strength of your indigo vat. A light sagebrush shade is best achieved in an older indigo vat that's yielding light blues, so this is a color that you have to wait for, and a good incentive to study and practice vat maintenance. Darker, more teal-like shades will be achieved

overdyeing

Once a fabric has been successfully mordanted and dyed, it does not need to be mordanted again if you want to overdye it. I don't do much overdyeing, but occasionally use it as a tool to transform colors I find uninspiring. If you create a color you're unhappy with, think of ways you can transform it to make it a color you will be inspired to use in your work.

Ripe peach on the left + dusty peach from the exhaust bath on the right

FORMULA 20: PEACH

The first piece of fabric out of this bath is the color of a ripe juicy peach, and the exhaust bath makes a lovely dusty peach color.

Make a tannin bath with gall tannin extract at 10% WOF, steeping for 12 to 24 hours. Mordant with potassium aluminum sulfate at 12% WOF, steeping for 24 hours. Weigh out the osage wood chips to 10% WOF. Weigh out finely ground madder root at 7.5% WOF. Fill the dye pot with enough hot tap water to submerge the fabric, and add the osage and madder plus the tiniest pinch of ground cochineal or cochineal extract. Stir to combine. Submerge the fabric in the dye bath. Slowly heat the bath to 170°F (75°C). Hold the dye bath at temperature for 1 hour, stirring occasionally and keeping the fibers submerged. Rinse and dry the fabric according to the directions on page 80. The exhaust bath can be used to create an ombré gradation. Hold each subsequent piece at 170°F (75°C) for one hour. When done dyeing, dispose of the dye bath according to the recommendations on page 37.

FINAL RINSING

To me, rinsing is the most tedious step in the natural dye process!

As fabric is extracted from the dye pot, rinse it once or twice in cold water to remove the bulk of any unaffixed dye, and then hang it to dry out of direct sunlight. Once dry, put the fabric in your rinse queue, but wait at least a week to give the natural dye time to cure on the fabric before doing the final rinses. Fill a bucket with warm water, add a small amount of natural liquid pH-neutral detergent and let the fabric soak for about 15 minutes, agitating it every so often. After that first rinse, cold water can be used for the remaining rinses. It'll take several rinses—sometimes a dozen or two—before the rinse water begins to run clear enough for the fabric to be safely used in a quilt. Be impeccable with your rinsing to avoid color bleeding. For assurance purposes, you may choose to do a final wash in the machine with a piece of white fabric as a test. If there's no bleed-off onto the white, your rinsing is good to go. After the final rinses are complete, hang the fabric to dry, then press it before folding it up and storing it in a dark place.

Dye Journal

I've learned so much about the art and alchemy of natural dyes by reading books, taking classes, and gleaning information wherever I can, but my most valuable lessons have come through personal experimentation and taking detailed notes along the way. I reference my dye journals constantly and always have one open in the studio. My journal is specific to the colors and WOF ratios and DOS that my water and my alchemy will provide. There's no dye book more valuable to me than my own journals. Any type of sketchbook works well. Whenever you begin a process, write it down: the weight and type of fabric, the type and amount of tannin and mordant, the WOF ratio, how you extracted the dye, the temperature you held it at and to what duration, etc. Include any lessons you learned. Once you've rinsed the dyed fabric, cut off a little swatch and affix it to your journal next to the notes on it. If you're doing an overdye, include a "before" swatch and an "after" swatch. I like to affix samples with hot glue, or tacky glue.

Peach/coral trials

oakgall → alum → 25% madder
                        cordial fica

① heat dye water to warm
   add madder + weld, cook 5min add cal
   add warm wetted fibers
   cook 1 hour

② Now reverse to 50% osage 10% madder
   too strong on osage I think try:

   dye base is   20%   5% madder
   taking up
   quickly, not   ③   add 5% more madder
   letting red
   penetrate
   fibers   + 5% more =

   ③ Added el cochineal   20% + 15% + 25%
                           osage   madder cal/c
   my fiber for 1 hour   5% of cor cal c

CATHY'S MAPLE STAR COLOR STORY

Cutch

Cutch

Myrobalan
Indigo

Myrobalan
Indigo

3.
quilt alchemy

Winter on the farm is a time for much-needed rest and planning out the next growing season, for tending the fire, mending broken things, and especially for making quilts from the rainbow of colors that were dyed on hot summer days—the colors of summer captured in cloth. The farm has given me an appreciation for winter in all its slowness. Those short days fly by, one after another, and soon enough become longer days that usher in spring, and the cycle begins again.

My desire to create feels involuntary, and making things is my favorite form of self-care. Creativity is an inherent human trait, but the distractions and demands of the modern world often rob us of it. Objects made by human hands are special and unique and incomparable to things that are mass manufactured.

I began garment sewing well before I began quilt making. In my head, quilting was a difficult task that I would work up to *someday*. When my garment-sewing scrap basket reached the point of overflowing and I couldn't part with the special scraps from all the clothes I had made for my kids over the years, that *someday* arrived, and my first quilt was born.

QUILT-MAKING SUPPLIES

Folks have been making beautiful quilts for hundreds of years without fancy tools. Scissors, pins, needles, thread, a measuring tape, and a thimble is how it all began. There are all kinds of modern tools made for quilters, and they're probably great, but I tend to stick with the basics. A well-made pair of tailor's shears that are used exclusively for fabrics, a rotary cutter, mat, and a quilter's ruler are what I use to cut my fabric for piecing. I also

have some square rulers in a couple of different sizes that are nice for trimming blocks. An iron is essential. Any iron will do, but I prefer a dry iron because there are no steam holes on the soleplate to get caught on seams. In place of steam, I use a spray bottle when needed. A sewing machine is an investment and there are so many options. I prefer a straight-stitch mechanical machine with an automatic thread cutter. Of course, you can opt to do the piecing by hand if you don't want to use a sewing machine.

- tailor's shears
- thread snips
- self-healing mat
- rotary cutter
- cutting ruler(s)
- seam ripper
- water-soluble marking tools
- tailor's tape
- glass head pins
- sewing machine
- iron
- ironing board or pressing pad
- ¼-inch seam marker ruler
- mechanical pencil
- square rulers

Opposite: **1.** Quilter's ruler **2.** ¼-inch seam marker **3.** mechanical pencil **4.** glass head pins **5.** tailor's tape **6.** thread snips **7.** marking tools **8.** seam ripper **9.** rotary cutter **10.** tailor's shears **11.** iron

SELECTING A PALETTE

Often one of the first steps in designing a quilt is selecting a palette, and a good palette is everything! When working with naturally dyed fabrics, we have nature on our side, because natural colors don't often clash—but that's not to say that you can put any naturally dyed colors together and have a palette that sings. Palette selection happens in all kinds of ways for me. Sometimes it's inspired by something I see in nature, or in town, or a painting. Sometimes I have a color fresh out of the dye pot that I'm inspired by, and that's my starting point. I put it next to other colors to see what will work with it and make my decisions based entirely on feeling. How does it feel when I put it next to this color? If I love it, and it feels right, I stick with it; if I'm uncertain, that's a no. I keep auditioning colors until the palette feels right. It's so interesting how adding or subtracting just one color will change the feeling immensely. Although often I select a palette first and base the design on what will make it sparkle, other times it's the design that comes first and the colors are selected according to what will accentuate that design. For reference, each quilt pattern includes the color formulas I used, but please select your personal palettes based on the colors you love.

SEAM ALLOWANCE

The standard seam allowance for piecing quilts is ¼ inch (6 mm). All of the following projects require a ¼-inch (6 mm) seam allowance unless otherwise stated.

patchwork squares quilt

I'm partial to patchwork square quilts because this is where my love for quilt making began. The simple square offers the beginner a perfect introduction to the most basic principles of cutting and sewing pieces together and matching seams. As simple as the construction of a patchwork square quilt is, I find that selecting colors for it can be a challenge.

The simplicity of this design offers a great opportunity to feature an ombré gradation. To do this, choose your favorite color recipe and create an ombré gradation of six varying hues. Once the gradation is achieved, either keep it as it is or modify it with iron or indigo. Then think about what color background will make your gradation sparkle and shine. Of course plain white is an option. I have a lot of dyed fabric in my stash, so I had the opportunity to audition my ombré squares on a few different colored backgrounds. When I began laying them out on the sagebrush background, I knew right away that it was the one! When auditioning colors and designs, it helps a ton to snap photos with your phone so you can see things from a reduced perspective. The finished size of this quilt is 48 by 48 inches (122 by 122 cm). If you would like to size it up or down, simply make more or fewer blocks, or increase or decrease the size of the squares.

FINISHED SIZE

- 48 by 48 inches (122 by 122 cm)

BLOCKS

- Finished blocks: 8 inches (20 cm)
- Total number of blocks: 36

PALETTE & MATERIALS

These instructions reflect the color choices I made for this quilt. I encourage you to choose your favorite color recipe and create an ombré gradation of six varying hues to use in place of those listed, for a personal, custom quilt.

Quilt top

- Six ½-yard (46 cm) pieces dyed with an ombré gradation consisting of 6 hues of osage gold (Formula 6), overdyed with indigo (see page 64) to shift it to greens
- 2 yards (183 cm) dyed sagebrush (Formula 19)

Backing, batting & binding

- 2 yards (183 cm) backing fabric: medium-strength indigo-dyed cotton (see page 62) overdyed with osage gold (Formula 6)
- 50 by 50-inch (127 by 127 cm) piece batting
- 100 m Japanese sashiko PFD dyed madder root red (Formula 1)
- ½ yard (46 cm) binding fabric: remnants of the osage gold gradient shifted in a 2% iron bath (see page 37)

CUT

- The squares are cut at 2½ inches. Cut 144 squares from your background color. Then cut 144 squares from your six ombré gradation shades. To make it easy you could cut 24 squares from each of the six shades, but I encourage you to put some thought into this and mix your colors up in a way that inspires you. For example, if you have one color from your gradation that stands out from the others, it could be used as a pop color only six times. Or maybe you want to use the pop color several times? Have fun with this, and experiment with moving the colors around until it feels right. Arrange the squares on the design wall or floor and play with the design before committing to sewing them together into blocks.

1. Lay out the blocks. Each block consists of eight gradation color squares and eight background squares. Arrange them into four rows, alternating gradation and background colors.

2. Sew the squares into four rows, pressing the seams open.

3. Matching the seams, sew the rows together, pressing the seams open.

4. Repeat steps 1 through 3 to make a total of 36 blocks.

5. Arrange the blocks on your design wall or floor, making six rows of six blocks each.

6. Matching the seams, sew the blocks together to make six horizontal rows, pressing the seams open.

7. Matching the seams, sew the rows together, pressing the seams open.

8. Make the quilt back following the directions on page 161.

9. Make the quilt sandwich following the directions on page 164.

10. Quilt the layers together following the directions on page 165.

11. Bind the quilt following the directions on page 168.

NOTE: If this project is your first try at quilt making, you will want to review the instructions in the Quilt-Making Skills chapter on page 138.

buffalo check version

Layout of the buffalo check version blocks

This version offers a fun opportunity to practice creating different depths of shade on different base fabrics of natural unwhitened linen and whitened linen. Choose any color recipe, and dye 1 yard (1 m) of unwhitened linen. Then use the exhaust bath to dye 1 yard (1 m) of white linen. I chose sagebrush (Formula 19). After treating both fabrics in the myrobalan tannin bath, I dipped the dark linen three times in my weak indigo vat, and the white linen twice. There are no exact rules on how to achieve the two depths of shade; you just have to do whatever it takes to achieve a significant difference in value between the light and the dark. Taking a black-and-white photo of your two shades next to each other will help you determine if there's enough of a difference in value. If the two shades look the same in black-and-white, you'll need to work on making one darker. Instead of using unwhitened linen, you could pre-treat your white fabric with a dark tannin to get that darker shade base. There are many possibilities, and that's what this experiment is intended to inspire. The squares are sewn into sixteen-patch blocks, as explained in the patchwork quilt instructions (see page 91).

tumbleweed quilt

This quilt was inspired by a photograph of a nineteenth-century doll quilt I came across. The shapes that make up this quilt are the four-patch, the QST (quarter-square triangle, aka the hourglass), and the HST (half-square triangle). These three shapes are the most fundamental pieces found within simple traditional quilt blocks. Together they can be arranged in different ways to create various star blocks, bear claws, and so many other quilt blocks. Re-creating vintage quilts is a great way to learn and build your skill set. Once you've re-created some quilts, you may be ready and inspired to design your own blocks.

I chose gray as my dominant color on a natural cotton background. This palette was inspired by the bleak colors of the high desert in wintertime—the colors of sagebrush and the winter trees and sky, the tumbleweeds that blow across the road on my drive home from trips to town. The black sawtooth border represents the biting cold and the feeling of being encapsulated by long, dark winter nights. Please be free to choose your own palette that has meaning to you.

The instructions provide the total amount of squares needed to make the blocks and border, and also the yardage of the colors I chose, but the challenge I offer here is for you to put some thought into your colors and how many squares of each color you cut, and how you arrange them. Have fun with this! The instructions are for a twin-size quilt. To size up or down, make more or fewer blocks accordingly.

FINISHED SIZE

- 64 × 88 inches (162.5 × 223.5 cm), which fits a twin bed

BLOCKS

- Finished blocks: 8 inches (20 cm)
- Total number of blocks: 70 (35 four-patch blocks and 35 four-patch hourglass blocks)

PALETTE & MATERIALS

Tumbleweed palette

- 1 yard (91 cm) dyed black (Formula 15)
- 1 yard (91 cm) worth dyed mixed grays from the black exhaust bath gradient
- ¼ yard (23 cm) dyed dark indigo (Formula 7)
- ¼ yard (23 cm) dyed light indigo (Formula 7)
- ¼ yard (23 cm) dyed cutch (Formula 9), strong dye bath
- ¼ yard (23 cm) dyed cutch (Formula 9), exhaust dye bath
- ½ yard (46 cm) dyed sagebrush (Formula 19)
- 2 yards (183 cm) natural organic cotton muslin
- ¼ yard (23 cm) mixed stripe prints from my garment sewing scrap basket

Backing, batting & binding

- 4 yards (3.6 m) backing fabric: various fabrics from my natural-dye stash

- Twin-size organic cotton batting
- 200 m sashiko thread white or any color of choice
- 1 yard (91 cm) binding fabric: dyed gray (Formula 15)

CUT

- **For the hourglass blocks** cut 5½-inch (14 cm) squares. Cut 70 natural undyed cotton squares (feel free to mix in some light colored prints, as I did). Then cut 70 mixed color squares from the tumbleweed palette. You may choose to cut an even amount of each color, or feel free to use more or less of any color.

- **For the four-patch blocks** cut 4½-inch (11 cm) squares. There's a total of 140 squares. Cut 70 undyed cotton squares (feel free to mix in some light-colored prints, as I did!) and 70 mixed color squares from the tumbleweed palette. Again, you may choose to cut an even amount of squares from each color, or feel free to use more or less of any color.

- **For the sawtooth border** cut 5-inch (12 cm) squares. Cut 34 natural undyed cotton squares, and 34 black squares. You will notice that I mixed in some light stripe prints with my white squares and mixed in a few gray squares with my black. There are no rules other than to have fun. In each corner of the border there is a natural cotton square, and these 4 squares are cut at 4½ inches (11 cm).

1. Make 140 QSTs following the directions on page 150, pairing the 5½-inch (14 cm) natural cotton squares with the 5½-inch (14 cm) hourglass color squares. Trim each QST to 4½ inches (11 cm).

2. Make 35 four-patch blocks with the 4½-inch (11 cm) squares following the directions on page 147.

3. Make 35 four-patch blocks with the QSTs, orienting them as shown in the photos.

4. Arrange the blocks on your design wall or floor into ten rows of seven blocks each, alternating hourglass blocks and four-patch blocks. Make sure you're happy with the flow of colors before sewing the blocks together. Taking photos on your phone helps!

5. Matching the seams, sew the blocks into ten rows, pressing the seams open.

6. Matching the seams, sew the rows together, pressing the seams open.

7. Make 68 HSTs following the directions on page 148, pairing the 5-inch (12 cm) black and 5-inch (12 cm) natural cotton squares together. Trim each HST to 4½ inches (11 cm).

I arranged my squares on the design wall before committing to sewing them into blocks.

8. Arrange the HSTs along the perimeter of the quilt to decide how you want to orient them as a sawtooth border. Place the 4½-inch (11 cm) natural squares in the corners.

9. Sew twenty HSTs together to form a vertical strip.

10. Matching the seams, sew the border to the side of the quilt top.

11. Repeat steps 9 and 10 for the other side.

12. Sew the fourteen HSTs plus two corner squares together to form a horizontal strip.

13. Matching the seams, sew the border to the bottom of the quilt top.

14. Repeat steps 12 and 13 for the top of the quilt top.

15. Make the quilt back following the directions on page 161.

16. Make the quilt sandwich following the directions on page 164.

17. Quilt the layers together following the directions on page 165.

18. Bind the quilt following the directions on page 168.

Arrangement of the sawtooth border

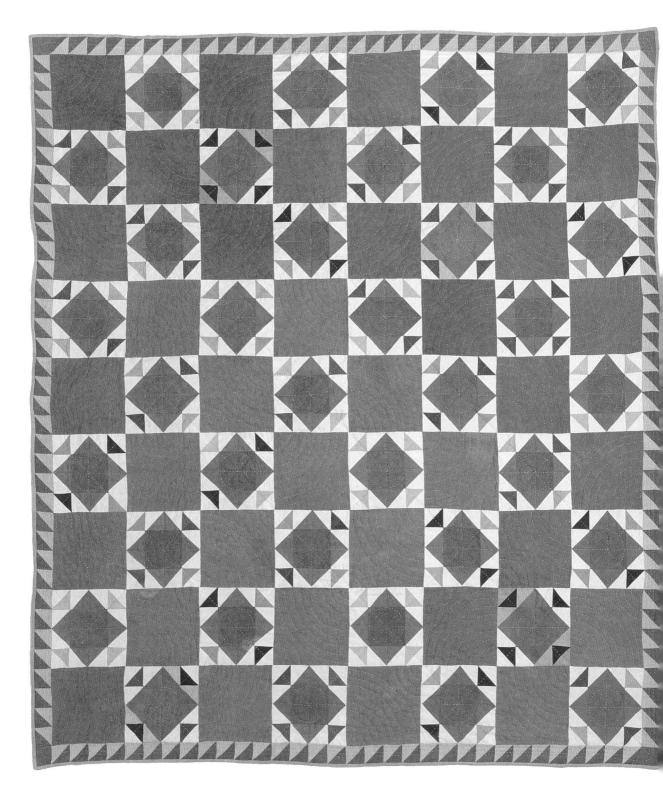

an ode to summer

The red and pink colors of madder root on a lush background of green give me all the summer feelings. With this variation of the traditional Jack in the Pulpit block, I want to introduce you to one final foundational shape commonly found within quilt blocks: the flying goose. The other shapes found within this version of the Jack in the Pulpit block are HSTs (half-square triangles) and squares. You may notice that two HSTs can be positioned to form the flying goose shape, and that's surely an option if you'd rather—there are often many different ways to construct a shape within a block.

This block also looks fantastic on a natural, undyed background, which would require much less dye work. To size this quilt up or down, simply make more or fewer blocks accordingly.

FINISHED SIZE

- To fit a queen-size bed (96 by 86 inches/244 by 218 cm)

BLOCKS

- Finished blocks: 10 inches (25 cm)
- Total blocks: 72 (36 Jack in the pulpit blocks and 36 spacer blocks)

PALETTE & MATERIALS

Quilt top

- 5 yards (4.5 m) background color: organic cotton-hemp blend fabric dyed olive green. Color recipe included in the osage recipe (Formula 6)
- 1 yard (91 cm) undyed white organic cotton-hemp blend
- 1 yard (91 cm) dyed madder pink (Formula 2)
- ½ yard (46 cm) dyed madder root red (Formula 1)

Backing, batting & binding

- 5 yards (4.5 m) backing fabric
- Queen-size batting
- 400 m hand-quilting thread
- 1 yard (91 cm) binding fabric: dyed sagebrush (Formula 19)

CUT

HSTs

- 72 3½-inch (9 cm) squares white
- 36 3½-inch (9 cm) squares madder pink
- 36 3½-inch (9 cm) squares madder red

Geese

- 36 6½-inch (16.5 cm) squares olive
- 144 3¾-inch (9.5 cm) squares white (make a few in a color for a fun pop!)

Jack in the Pulpit center squares

- 36 5½-inch (14 cm) squares olive

Spacer blocks

- 36 10½-inch (26.5 cm) squares olive

Sawtooth border

- 68 3½-inch (9 cm) squares madder pink
- 68 3½-inch (9 cm) squares olive
- 4 3-inch (7.5 cm) squares olive for corners

1+2

1. Make 144 flying geese following the directions on page 151, using the 6½-inch (16.5 cm) olive squares and 3¾-inch (9.5 cm) white squares. Trim the geese to 3 by 5½ inches (7.5 by 14 cm).

2. Make 144 HSTs following the directions on page 148, pairing the 3½-inch (9 cm) white squares with the madder pink and madder red squares. Trim the HSTs to 3 inches (7.5 cm).

3. Arrange the block pieces as shown to make a Jack in the Pulpit block, placing the 5½-inch (14 cm) olive squares in the centers.

4. Sew the pieces into horizontal rows, pressing the seams open.

5. Matching the seams, sew the rows together and press the seams open to make a completed block.

TIP

For faster piecing, it helps to come up with a system. My system began by sewing a flying goose to both sides of each of the 36 center squares to create all 36 of the middle rows. Then I sewed a HST to each side of the remaining flying geese, being careful to keep all the shapes oriented in the correct directions. Once all the rows were created, I pinned a top and bottom row to each middle row.

10. Make 136 HSTs following the directions on page 148, pairing the 3½-inch (9 cm) madder pink and 3½-inch (9 cm) olive squares together. Trim each HST to 3 inches (7.5 cm).

11. Arrange the HSTs along the perimeter of the quilt to decide how you want to orient them as a sawtooth border. Place the 3-inch (7.5 cm) olive squares in the corners.

12. Sew thirty-six HSTs together to form a vertical strip.

13. Matching the seams, sew the border to the side of the quilt top.

14. Repeat steps 12 and 13 for the other side.

15. Sew the 32 HSTs plus two corner squares together to form a horizontal strip.

16. Matching the seams, sew the border to the bottom of the quilt top.

17. Repeat steps 15 and 16 for the top of the quilt top.

18. Make the quilt back following the directions on page 161.

19. Make the quilt sandwich following the directions on page 164.

20. Quilt the layers together following the directions on page 165.

21. Bind the quilt following the directions on page 168.

6. Repeat steps 3 through 5 to make a total of 36 blocks.

7. Arrange the blocks on your design wall or floor, making nine rows of eight blocks each, beginning with a pieced block in the top left corner and alternating olive green spacer blocks. Move the blocks around until the design flows, especially with the variance in the shades of madder red. I almost always make a few unique blocks that are slightly different from the rest to add visual interest to a quilt, too.

8. Matching the seams, sew the blocks together to make nine rows, pressing the seams open.

9. Matching the seams, sew the rows together, pressing the seams open.

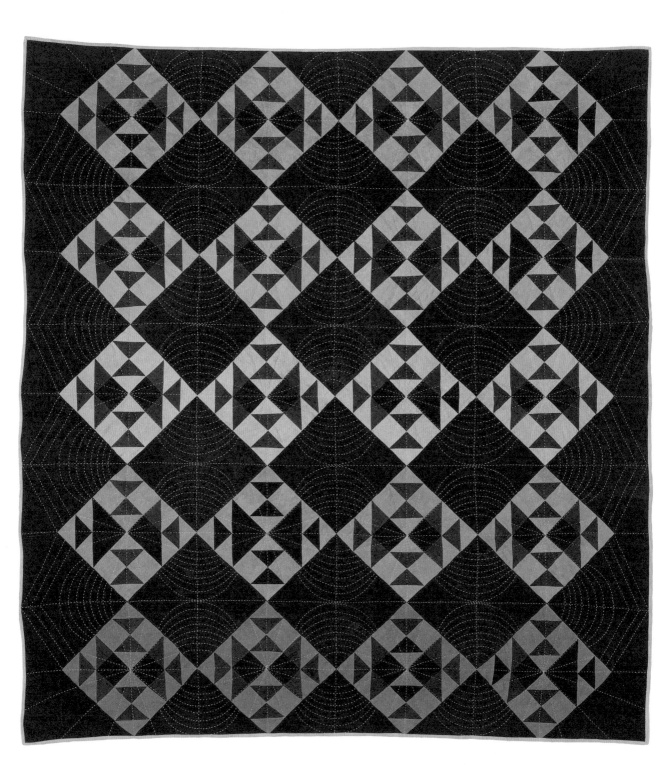

jackrabbit quilt

One night as my daughter and I were driving home from town, we came upon two jackrabbits running down the middle of the road. They ran in front of our car for a mile or more, zigzagging and crossing each other so gracefully, like a choreographed dance, their huge ears luminescent in the headlights. It was a moment so magical that it felt like time slowed down for us to take it in. This traditional Old Maid's Puzzle quilt block gave me an opportunity to capture that moment in quilt form.

A dark night background and geometric shapes to represent those zigzagging jackrabbits illuminated in the headlights make up each block. The block is simple to make from only squares and HSTs, but the skill I wish to introduce here is in setting blocks on point: orienting a block as a diamond shape ("on point") rather than a square will make certain blocks, like this one, more visually interesting and dynamic. It's a good skill to have in your tool kit.

Here also is an opportunity to create several yards of beautiful naturally dyed black fabric as a dark night background. This is a big quilt that will fit on a king-size bed. To size this one down, you could either make fewer blocks or decrease the size of the blocks. If you wish to change the size of the HSTs, the HST tutorial on page 148 explains how to make them in any size. The quilt math for on-point blocks is explained in the on-point tutorial on page 157.

FINISHED SIZE

- To fit a queen- or king-size bed (91 by 99 inches/231 by 251 cm)

BLOCKS

- Finished blocks: 14 inches (35.5 cm)
- Total number of blocks: 32 (20 old maid's puzzle piece blocks and 12 black spacer blocks)

PALETTE & MATERIALS

Quilt top

- 6 yards (5.5 m) dyed black (Formula 15)
- 1 yard (91 cm) dyed quebracho (Formula 10) at 15% WOF
- 1 yard (91 cm) dyed quebracho (Formula 10) using the exhaust bath
- 1 yard (91 cm) dyed black walnut brown (Formula 12) at 10% WOF
- 1 yard (91 cm) dyed Himalayan rhubarb (Formula 11) at 20% WOF
- 1 yard (91 cm) dyed Himalayan rhubarb (Formula 11) using the exhaust bath

Backing, batting & binding

- 6 yards (5.5 m) backing fabric: consider using your exhaust baths to dye fabric for the backing
- King-size batting
- 400 m hand-quilting thread
- 1 yard (91 cm) binding fabric dyed black walnut (Formula 12) using the exhaust bath

CUT

- 100 4½-inch (11 cm) squares black
- 20 4½-inch (11 cm) squares each of the five "headlight" colors
- 40 4-inch (10 cm) squares black
- 16 4-inch (10 cm) squares each of the five "headlight" colors
- 12 14½-inch (37 cm) squares black
- 4 21⅛-inch (51 cm) squares black
- 2 11-inch (28 cm) squares black
- 2 6-inch (15 cm) strips black, length to be determined

The jackrabbit block layout (see step 2)

The jackrabbit blocks on my design wall. The fifth row is on the ground because it won't fit on the wall.

108

1. Make 200 HSTs following the directions on page 148, pairing the 4½-inch (11 cm) black and 4½-inch (11 cm) "headlight" squares together. Trim each HST to 4 inches (10 cm).

2. Using the HSTs and solid 4-inch (10 cm) squares, arrange the block pieces as shown, in four rows of four squares each.

3. Sew the pieces into four rows, pressing the seams open.

4. Matching the seams, sew the rows together, pressing the seams open.

5. Arrange the blocks on your design wall or floor, making five rows (one of each color) of four blocks, orienting the blocks as diamonds.

6. Place a 14½-inch (37 cm) black square in each of the twelve open diamond spaces.

7. Cut each of the 21⅛-inch (51 cm) black squares diagonally from corner to corner and then again from the opposite corner to corner to make four side triangles. Place a side triangle in each of the fourteen open triangle spaces along the perimeter of the quilt. (You will have two extra side triangles.)

8. Cut each of the two 11-inch (28 cm) black squares diagonally just once from corner to corner to make four corner triangles total.

9. Follow the on-point tutorial on page 157 to sew the blocks into diagonal rows.

10. Add a 6-inch (15 cm) wide border on each side of the quilt, referring to the border tutorial on page 159.

11. Make the quilt back following the directions on page 161.

12. Make the quilt sandwich following the directions on page 164.

13. Quilt the layers together following the directions on page 165.

14. Bind the quilt following the directions on page 168.

The blocks arranged in diagonal rows for an on-point setting with the side-setting triangles around the perimeter and corner triangles in the four corners

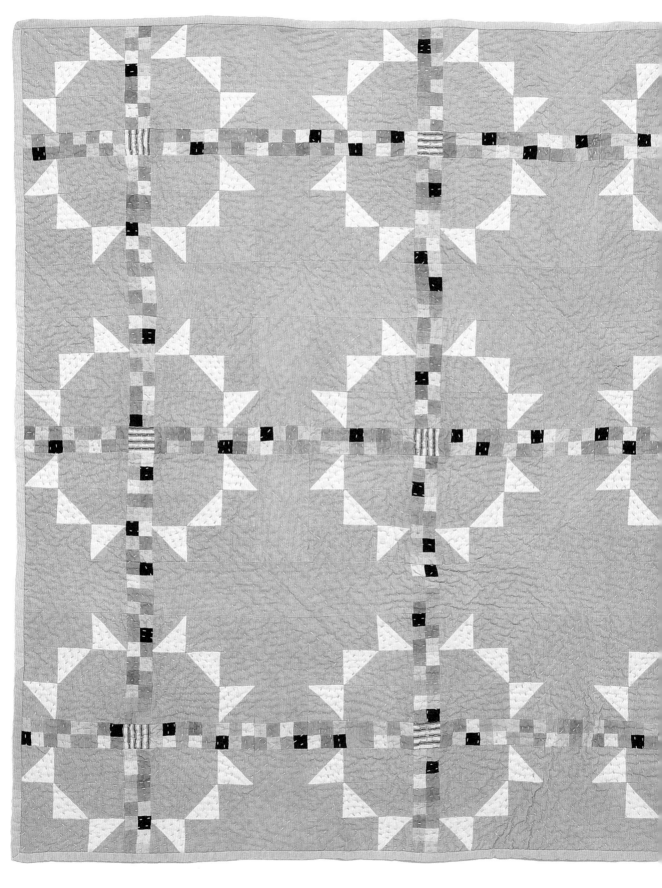

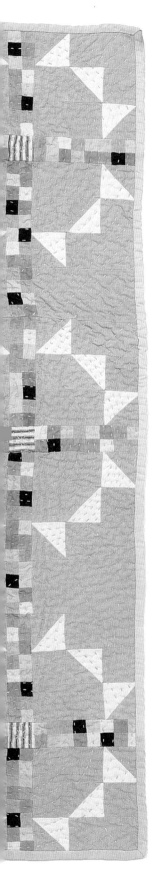

the mycelium quilt

Mycelium is incredibly tiny fungal threads that are interconnected to form massive mycelial networks or "wood wide webs." Water, nutrients, and minerals are transferred through this amazing network, and trees are able to communicate with each other through it. Mycelium is a beautiful example of interconnectedness. The white stars in this quilt represent individual trees that are connected by a mycelial network of tiny intricate fabric scraps. My intention with this pattern is to show you how to come up with your own quilt sketches. Once you're familiar with the most basic shapes I've introduced, you can use them to create your own unique blocks in any size. This is also an example of how to utilize small scraps, because naturally dyed scraps are too special not to use.

FINISHED SIZE

- 48 by 48 inches (122 by 122 cm)

BLOCKS

- Finished blocks: 14 inches (35.5 cm)
- Total number of blocks: 9

PALETTE & MATERIALS

Quilt top

- 1 yard (91 cm) natural undyed organic cotton-hemp blend
- Various dyed small scraps
- 2 yards (183 cm) dyed sagebrush (Formula 19)

Backing, batting & binding

- 2 yards (183 cm) backing fabric
- 52 by 52 inch (132 by 132 cm) piece batting

- Sashiko thread (100m) dyed madder pink (Formula 2)
- ½ yard (46 cm) binding fabric dyed madder pink (Formula 2)

CUT

- 54 3-inch (7.5 cm) squares sagebrush
- 54 3-inch (7.5 cm) squares undyed
- 72 2½-inch (6 cm) squares sagebrush
- 72 2½ by 4½-inch (6 by 11 cm) rectangles sagebrush
- 672 1¼-inch (3 cm) squares mixed scrap colors
- 16 6¼ by 3½-inch (16 by 9 cm) rectangles sagebrush
- 4 15 by 3½-inch (38 by 9 cm) rectangles sagebrush
- 9 2-inch (5 cm) squares stripes for block centers

1. Make 108 HSTs following the directions on page 148, pairing the 3-inch (7.5 cm) sagebrush and 3-inch (7.5 cm) natural cotton squares together. Trim each HST to 2½ inches (6 cm). Using the HSTs, solid 2½-inch (6 cm) sagebrush squares, and solid 2½ by 4½-inch (6 by 11 cm) sagebrush rectangles, arrange the four quadrants of each star block as shown, in three rows each.

2. Sew the pieces together to form twelve horizontal rows, three in each quadrant, pressing the seams open.

3. Matching the seams, sew the rows together to form four quadrants, pressing the seams open. Repeat steps 2 and 3 to make eight more blocks' worth of quadrants (thirty-six quadrants total).

4. Make the scrappy mycelium chains: Mix up your 672 scrappy 1¼-inch (3 cm) squares and sew squares together to make 336 pairs, pressing the seams open. Organize the pairs into thirty-six piles of eight and twelve piles of four. Sew each pile into strips to form thirty-six chains of eight pairs, and twelve chains of four pairs.

5. Arrange the pieces together as shown, with four quadrants (as finished in step 3), four eight-pair mycelium chains, and 2-inch (5 cm) striped center square.

6. Sew the pieces together to form three horizontal rows.

7. Matching the seams, sew the rows together, to finish the block, pressing the seams open. Repeat steps 5 through 7 to make nine star blocks total.

8. Make spacer blocks by sewing a scrappy mycelium chain between two 6¼ by 3½-inch (16 by 9 cm) sagebrush rectangles (as shown), pressing the seams open. Repeat until you have six spacer blocks.

9. Arrange three star blocks with a spacer block between each one. Matching the seams, sew them together, pressing the seams open. Repeat this step twice to create three rows.

10. Make two-row spacer strips by arranging three four-pair mycelium chains with two 6¼ by 3½-inch (16 by 9 cm) sagebrush rectangles and two 15 by 3½-inch (38 by 9 cm)

sagebrush rectangles, as shown. Sew this strip together, pressing the seams open. Repeat this step once more, so you have two spacer strips total.

11. To sew the quilt top: Arrange the star block strips and spacer strips as shown. Matching the seams, sew the columns together, pressing the seams open. Make the quilt back following the directions on page 161. Next, make the quilt sandwich following the directions on page 164. Last, quilt the layers together following the directions on page 165 and bind the quilt following the directions on page 168.

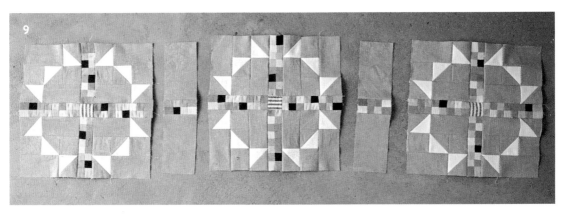

114

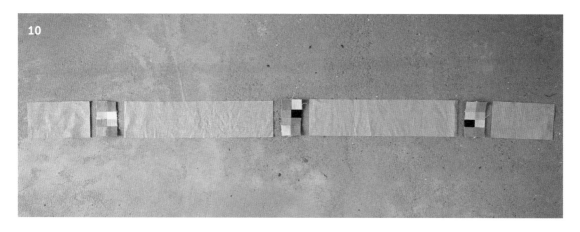

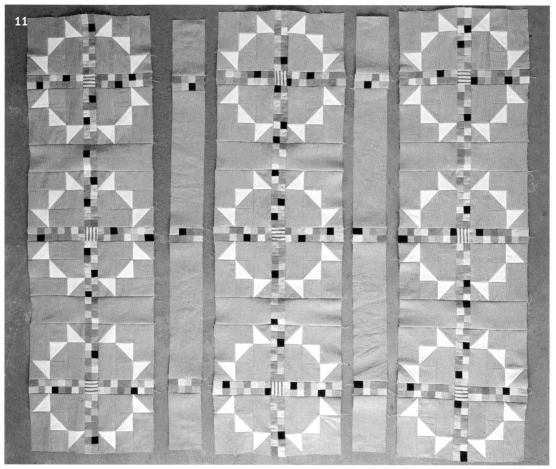

broken dishes quilt poncho

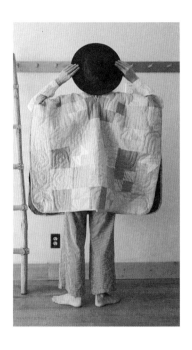

Broken Dishes is a traditional quilt block made from squares and HSTs dating back to at least the 1790s. This poncho features a simplified variation of the traditional block. Speaking of simple, this is about the simplest way to wear a quilt! If you're not so keen on the broken dishes block, go ahead and switch it up: Choose any block and make a quilt top that finishes somewhere around 42 inches wide (107 cm) by 72 inches long (183 cm). For a custom-size poncho, adjust these measurements accordingly. Choose something nice for the lining, because the poncho is reversible. I selected a palette of subtle neutrals that I created from Formula 13: Exhaust Bath Neutrals (page 72) along with some pastel shades that give this piece a vintage feel. The dark indigo-dyed lining provides the hand-quilted arches a platform to shine on.

FINISHED SIZE

- 42 by 72 inches (107 by 183 cm)

BLOCKS

- Finished blocks: 6 inches (15 cm)
- Total number of blocks: 84 (42 broken dishes blocks and 42 spacer blocks)

PALETTE & MATERIALS

Poncho top

- 2 yards (183 cm) various neutral shades (Formula 13)
- Remnant pieces of light indigo (Formula 7), sagebrush (Formula 19), natural undyed cotton, madder pink (Formula 2), vintage stripes, and calico prints

Lining, batting & binding

- 2¼ yards (206 cm) lining fabric dyed dark indigo (formula 7)
- 46 by 76-inch (117 by 193 cm) piece wool or cotton batting
- Hand-quilting thread
- ½ yard (46 cm) binding fabric

CUT

- 42 4-inch (10 cm) squares various neutral shades
- 42 4-inch (10 cm) squares various colors (light indigo, sagebrush, undyed, madder pink, stripes, calico)
- 84 3½-inch (9 cm) squares various neutral shades
- 42 6½-inch (16.5 cm) squares various neutral shades

1. Make 84 HSTs following the directions on page 148, pairing the 4-inch (10 cm) neutral squares and 4-inch (10 cm) colored squares together. Trim each HST to 3½ inches (9 cm).

2. Lay out the broken dishes blocks as shown in photo 1, and sew the pieces together as you would a four-patch block (see page 147).

3. Arrange the broken dishes blocks and the 6½-inch (16.5 cm) neutral squares on your design wall or floor, making twelve rows of seven blocks each, alternating pieced blocks and spacer blocks as shown. Move the blocks around until you're happy with the flow.

4. Sew the blocks into rows, pressing the seams open.

5. Matching the seams, sew the rows together, pressing the seams open.

6. Mark the V-neck opening: Locate the center of the quilt top by folding it in half lengthwise and then again widthwise or by following the seam lines. Use a marking tool to mark a cross at the center point. Then, with the quilt top oriented vertically, mark a vertical line 7 inches (17 cm) above the center mark and 7 inches (17 cm) below it as shown on page 120.

7. Make the quilt sandwich using the lining as the backing fabric following the directions on page 164.

8. Quilt the layers together following the directions on page 165.

9. Use a round object and a marking tool to round the poncho corners as shown in photo 9a (page 120). Cut along the marked lines as shown in 9b.

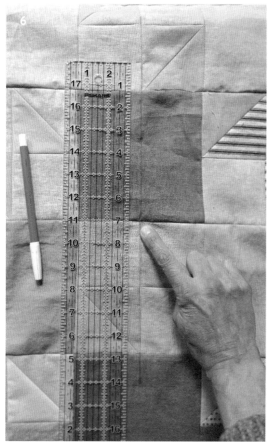

The patchwork side of the reversible poncho

The solid side of the poncho

10. Bind the outer edge of the poncho following the directions on page 168.

11. Cut the V-neck opening along the line made in step 6 with a ruler and rotary cutter. Try the poncho on to see how it fits; cut the opening a little bigger if need be. Set your sewing machine stitch length to around 1.5

and staystitch ⅛-inch (3 mm) from the edge of the opening to secure any hand quilting that may have been cut.

12. Bind the V-neck following the binding directions on page 168. When you come to the point of the V, open the V out as shown and sew the binding on in a straight line.

tiny quilts:
a hand-quilting
study

These tiny quilts are a great way to use up scraps and to practice improvisational piecing and different hand stitches. If you're new to hand quilting, here's an opportunity to give it a try before committing to a big quilt. Have fun with these and let yourself be free to combine colors and stitches that you wouldn't normally try. New discoveries are often made in those unexpected ways. Leave off the loop if you prefer to frame them.

FINISHED SIZE

- Varies

1. Gather your scraps. I grouped mine into mono-chromatic piles.

2. Lay out the scraps in a way that makes sense to sew them together and trim them up if necessary.

3. Start sewing the scraps together. When improv piecing, there's no right or wrong way to do it. Simply work with what you have and figure out a logical way to sew the pieces together. Sew scraps together until it is as large as you'd like or about 9½ by 9½ inches (24 by 24 cm).

4. Trim the pieced fabric to 9½ by 9½ inches (24 by 24 cm) or whatever size you desire.

5. Create a second piece for the back the same way, or cut a 9½ by 9½-inch (24 by 24 cm) piece of fabric.

6. Hand quilt the piece in any way that inspires you. Hand ties are another wonderful option.

7. When you make the binding tape according to the directions on page 168, make an extra 8 inches (20 cm) to use as a loop. To make the loop, fold the 8-inch piece of binding tape in half lengthwise and press. Open it up and fold both raw edges to the fold line and press. Fold this in half, then topstitch along the open side to enclose it.

8. Align the raw edges of the loop at the middle of the top edge of the tiny quilt as shown and sew in place with a ⅛-inch (3 mm) seam allowance. Bind the quilt following the directions on page 168, enclosing the loop ends in the binding.

9. Hand stitch the binding with the loop facing down. When finished, press the loop up.

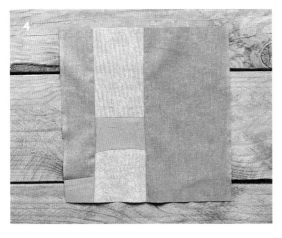

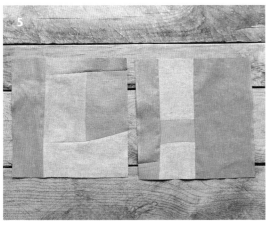

hand-quilting tool roll

Here's a pattern for a fun patchwork tool roll to keep all of your hand-quilting tools tidy and together in one place. I keep only the most essential tools in my roll, including a small pair of snips, a thimble, quilting needles, marking tools, safety pins, a hera marker, and a small ruler. Needles can be stored on the wool felt flap that also serves as a pocket where I keep safety pins and my thimble. These instructions explain how to make a tool roll from the snowball block, but feel free to choose a different block if you please. The finished patchwork dimensions are 18 by 12 inches (46 by 30.5 cm); you could make any patchwork panel that size.

FINISHED SIZE

- 18 by 12 inches (46 by 30.5 cm)

BLOCKS

- Finished blocks: 3 inches (7.5 cm)
- Total number of blocks: 24

PALETTE & MATERIALS

- Scraps of natural undyed cotton
- Scraps of dyed black (Formula 15)
- Tiny scraps of dyed cutch (Formula 9)
- 12½ by 18½-inch (32 by 47 cm) piece dyed light indigo (Formula 7) for the lining
- 5¼ by 18½-inch (13 by 47 cm) piece striped fabric for the pocket
- Small piece wool felt for the pocket flap

CUT

- 12 3½-inch (9 cm) squares white
- 12 3½-inch (9 cm) squares black
- 43 1½-inch (4 cm) squares white
- 43 1½-inch (4 cm) squares black
- 10 1½-inch (4 cm) contrast color squares
- 1 12½ by 18½-inch (32 by 47 cm) rectangle batting
- 1 12½ by 18½-inch (32 by 47 cm) rectangle indigo for pouch lining
- 1 5¼ by 18½-inch (13 by 47 cm) rectangle in stripes for pocket
- 1 28-inch (71 cm) length ³⁄₁₆-inch (5 mm) flat leather lacing
- 1 5 by 8-inch (12 by 20 cm) rectangle wool felt

128

1. Make 12 black snowball blocks and 12 white snowball blocks following the directions on page 154, using the 3½-inch (9 cm) squares and 1½-inch (4 cm) corner squares.

2. Arrange the snowball squares in four rows of six blocks each, alternating black and white snowball blocks.

3. Matching the seams, sew the blocks together to make four rows, pressing the seams open.

4. Matching the seams, sew the rows together, pressing the seams open.

5. Place the finished patchwork top right side up on top of the piece of batting. Smooth out all the wrinkles and baste the two layers together with safety pins (see page 164).

6. Hand quilt the two layers together (see page 165).

7. Place the piece of wool felt on top of the lining fabric, aligning the raw edges at the bottom and placing it 3 inches (7.5 cm) from the right edge. Pin it in place, then baste the bottom edge to the lining ¼ inch (6 mm) from the edge.

8. Fold down the top edge of the pocket fabric first ¼ inch (6 mm) then ½ inch (12 mm), pressing well with each fold. Pin in place.

9. Set your stitch length to 3 and topstitch the pocket along the fold.

10. Pin the pocket to the lining, matching the raw edges on the left, right, and bottom edges, with wrong side to right side as shown. Sew the pocket to the lining ¼ inch (6 mm) from the raw edges on the sides and bottom.

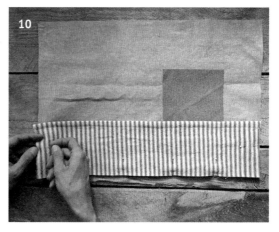

11. Topstitch the pocket along both edges of the wool felt to hold it in place. (See page 129.)

12. Topstitch custom pocket slot openings depending on the size of your personal tools.

13. Place the patchwork piece right side up on your work surface. Then overlap the pocket flap on it. Make a mark with tailor's chalk or any marking tool just above the top of the hemmed pocket edge.

14. Place the leather strap on the mark you made, aligning the raw edge of the strap and the patchwork. Tape it to the patchwork to keep it in place as shown and sew it in place ¼ inch (6 mm) from the edge, going back and forth a few times to secure it well.

15. Place the lining on top of the patchwork, right sides together. Use a round object and a marking tool to mark cutting lines to round the corners and cut along the lines through all layers.

16. Pin the lining to the patchwork and sew the layers together along the perimeter ½ inch (12 mm) from the raw edges, leaving a 3-inch (7.5 cm) opening unsewn on the top edge. Trim the seam allowance to ¼ inch (6 mm).

17. Turn the piece to the right side through the opening, pushing the corners out. Press gently. Press the opening seam allowance to the inside and hand-sew it neatly closed.

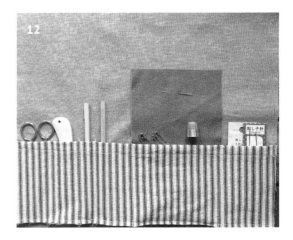

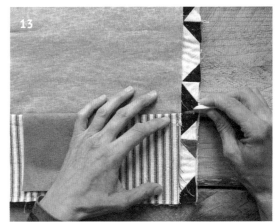

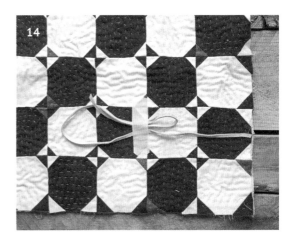

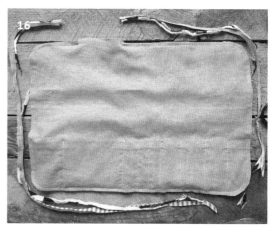

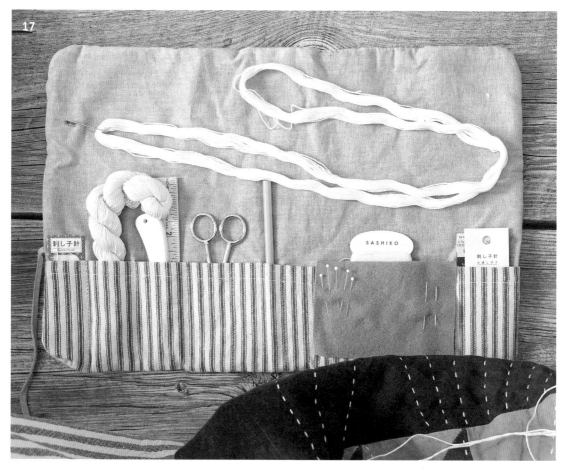

variable star quilted satchel

Variable star is a traditional American quilt block dating back to the early nineteenth century. I chose this block to show you how to make a star from QSTs and squares. This pattern is a very simple way to make a quilted bag. After you make your first one, you might choose to make another with a different quilt block or change the size of the block to make it smaller for children. If you're not a fan of a satchel, you can make two handles to turn this into a tote bag.

FINISHED SIZE

- 14½ by 18 inches (37 by 46 cm)

BLOCKS

- Finished blocks: 15 inches (38 cm)
- Total number of blocks: 2

PALETTE & MATERIALS

Quilted bag pieces and strap

- 1 yard (91 cm) dyed cutch 10% WOF (Formula 9)
- ¼ yard (23 cm) dyed cutch 35% WOF (Formula 9)
- ¼ yard (23 cm) natural undyed organic cotton

Lining, batting & strap

- ½ yard (46 cm) lining fabric of choice
- Scrap pieces of batting, approximately 20 inches square
- Hand-quilting thread

CUT

QSTs

- 4 6½-inch (16.5 cm) light cutch
- 4 6½-inch (16.5 cm) white

Solid squares

- 2 5½-inch (14 cm) dark cutch
- 8 5½-inch (14 cm) light cutch

Edging strips

- Four 2 by 15½-inch (5 by 39 cm) rectangles light cutch

Lining

- Two 15½ by 18-inch (39 by 46 cm) rectangles lining fabric

Batting

- Two 17 by 20-inch (43 by 50 cm) rectangles batting

Strap

- One 8½ by 40-inch (21.5 by 101 cm) rectangle light cutch. Note: The strap will be fitted to your body. For larger sizes, determine your strap length before cutting in case you want it longer.

1. Make 8 QSTs following the directions on page 150, pairing the 6½-inch (16.5 cm) white squares with the 6½-inch (16.5 cm) light cutch squares. Trim each QST to 5½ inches (14 cm).

2. Arrange the QSTs and solid 5½-inch (14 cm) squares to form the Ohio star block, placing a dark cutch square at the center and light cutch squares in the corners, as shown.

3. Sew the pieces together to make three rows, pressing the seams open.

4. Matching the seams, sew the rows together, pressing the seams open. Repeat steps 2 and 3 to make a second Ohio star block.

5. Sew the 2 by 15½-inch (5 by 39 cm) rectangles to the top and bottom of each block.

6. Place each finished patchwork top right side up on top of a piece of batting. Smooth out all the wrinkles and baste the two layers together with safety pins (see page 164).

7. Hand quilt the two layers together (see page 165).

8. Place the quilted panels on top of each other with right sides facing. Matching the seams, sew them together along the sides and bottom with a ¼-inch (6 mm) seam allowance. Repeat for the lining, pressing the seams open.

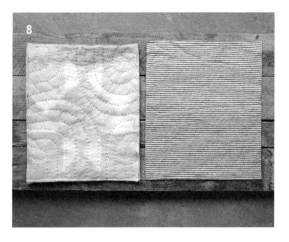

9. Open out the corners of the quilted piece as shown. Measure 1¼ inches (3 cm) from the tip of the corner and mark a line perpendicular to the seam. Press it to keep it in place, then sew across the line through all layers.

10. Trim the seam allowance to ¼ inch (6 mm). Repeat steps 9 and 10 with the lining.

11. Fold the strap in half lengthwise and press. Open it up and fold both raw edges to the fold line and press. Fold in half again (11a), then topstitch along the open side to enclose it (11b).

12. Insert the strap into the quilted bag, which is still wrong side out. Center the strap end over one side seam with raw edges aligned and pin in place. Make sure the strap isn't twisted and repeat at the other side. Sew the strap with a ¼-inch (6 mm) seam allowance, going back and forth over it a couple times to secure.

13. Insert the lining into the bag with the right sides facing. Matching side seams, align the raw edges. Sew the lining to the bag with a ½-inch (12 mm) seam allowance, leaving a 4-inch (10 cm) opening unsewn. When you come to the straps, sew back and forth a couple of times.

14. Turn the bag to the right side through the gap, then reach into the opening and push the corners out. Situate the lining in the bag. Press along the top edge of the bag, tucking the seam allowance of the opening in. Beginning at the gap, topstitch ¼ inch (6 mm) from the edge all the way around. Leave long tails, then make a quilter's knot (see page 166) with the ends and sink it between the top and batting layers.

4.
quilt-making skills

Here in the quilt-making skill section is a collection of tutorials for the most essential skills, presented in chronological quilt-making order. The quilt patterns refer you here often, but beyond that I hope you will use this section as a resource to turn to when you wish to sketch up blocks and quilts of your own. When I design quilts of my own, I often have to stop and google formulas for half square triangles and the other basic shapes that I've shared here. It usually takes a little while for me to remember which methods and formulas I prefer and where I last found them, so I'm personally really pleased to have them and all the other tutorials filed away together here in one convenient-to-access place.

FINISHED VERSUS UNFINISHED BLOCKS

In the world of quilting, the terms "finished" and "unfinished" appear a lot. "Finished" refers to the size of a quilt block or the pieces that make up a block *after* they've been sewn to other blocks or pieces. The term "unfinished" refers to the size of a block *before* it's been sewn to other blocks. In quilting, a ¼-inch (6 mm) seam allowance is standard, making unfinished blocks and pieces ½ inch (12 mm) larger than finished blocks (¼ inch on both sides along one dimension means ½ inch/12 mm extra fabric). It can be confusing at first, but don't overthink it. Determine what size you need your finished pieces to be, and simply add ½ inch (12 mm) to determine your unfinished size.

DETERMINING QUILT SIZES AND BLOCK SCALE

As a basic rule of thumb when determining what size quilt to make for a bed, measure the mattress and add approximately 2 feet (60 cm) to the width and 1 foot (12.5 cm) to the length. For more or less overhang, increase or decrease those measurements. Once those measurements are determined, they'll be used to calculate the size and number of quilt blocks needed. The ability to make quilt blocks in custom sizes provides an opportunity to change the scale of a design. An intricate quilt might contain hundreds of small blocks, and a minimalist quilt perhaps just four large blocks. Sometimes it helps to cut paper squares in various sizes to get a block size visual. To calculate the number of blocks needed, divide the quilt width by your desired block size, then round up or down accordingly. You may have to tweak your block size a little to get the math to work out, or reach your desired size by adding a border. The math for diagonal on-point (see page 157) settings is different because the diagonal measurement of a block is larger than its side-to-side measurement. I never fuss too much over a quilt being an exact size, but when in doubt I always round up. A quilt that's a little too big on a bed is so much better than a quilt that doesn't quite fit.

CUTTING WITH A ROTARY CUTTER

All of the shapes in this book are cut from squares, which are cut from strips. To cut strips, fold your fabric in half selvedge to selvedge. If your fabric is wrinkly give it a good press. Use a rotary cutter and quilter's ruler to trim a scant bit to even the fabric if necessary. Many hemp and linen fabrics are 58 inches (147 cm) wide, so it's handy to have a quilter's ruler and cutting mat that's at least 36 inches (91 cm) wide for cutting strips from those wider fabrics. Use your rotary cutter and ruler to cut strips at whatever width your squares need to be, then again to cut squares from the strips. It's important to cut very accurate pieces. I have two cutting rulers, one 4 by 36 inches (10 by 91 cm) for cutting strips, and one 6½ by 24 inches (16.5 by 61 cm) for cutting squares and other shapes from strips.

PIECING AND PRESSING SEAMS

When creating the shapes that make up quilt blocks, it's important to cut and match everything up as precisely as possible. To sew two squares together place them on top of each other with right sides facing (if your fabric isn't solid then it has a right and wrong side), lign up all the corners and edges, and pin along one edge to hold the squares in place. Sew along the pinned edge with a ¼-inch (6 cm) seam allowance, removing the pins right before you come to them. In quilt making it's really important to be diligent in keeping an accurate ¼-inch (6 mm) seam allowance. This is tricky at first, but with practice it becomes something you barely think about. After the pieces have been sewed together the seams must be pressed. When I first began quilting, I was taught that I *must* press all seams to the side, but then in a quilt class I took the instructor suggested pressing seams open for better accuracy, and I found it really helped, so I've stuck with it despite its being unorthodox. I encourage you to try both ways to see which works best for you.

MATCHING SEAMS

When sewing blocks and rows of blocks together, the seams are used as a place to match and pin everything together. For the best accuracy, take your time matching seams; this method ensures the seams are perfectly aligned. It will soon enough become effortless. When machine sewing, keep your needle in the down position and remove the pins right before you come to them.

1. With the patchwork right sides together and the raw edges and seams aligned, pierce both layers of fabric right between the open seams, about ½ inch (12 mm) from the raw edge.

2. Lift the top patchwork and ensure the pin is directly in the seam of both pieces of the patchwork. Then bring the pin back up through the seam to the top side.

3. All these seams are matched up and pinned neatly and the pieces are ready to be sewn together.

4. Note when viewed from the back side, the pins are all aligned perfectly with the seams.

Seams pressed open

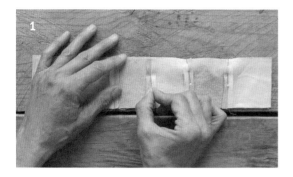

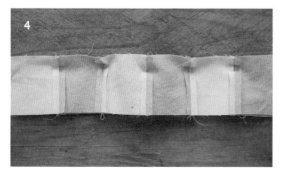

RE-CREATING TRADITIONAL QUILT BLOCKS

Many traditional quilts are made up of square blocks that are created one at a time and then joined together to become a quilt top. Some quilt blocks are complicated and intricate, consisting of many tiny shapes and pieces, but many are simple, requiring only squares and other basic shapes that can be arranged in varying ways to create different designs. Most of my quilts are made from simple traditional quilt blocks, and I often look to vintage quilts for inspiration. When observing a vintage quilt that I admire, I'll deconstruct it in my mind to identify the individual blocks. Once the blocks are identified I'll attempt to sketch one onto graph paper. Through this process of dissecting a block on graph paper I discover the shapes within the block. Some of the most common and versatile quilt piece shapes found within quilt blocks are the square, the half-square triangle (HST), the quarter-square triangle (QST), and the flying goose. Once you gain the ability to create these pieces in custom sizes, you'll be able to make many different quilt blocks on your own in any custom size without having to rely on a pattern. These simple pieces can be arranged in many different ways—to form star blocks and bear claws and many other traditional block designs. They can also be used to design blocks and borders of your own. Get to know the names of traditional quilt blocks. You'll soon discover that some blocks have two or more names. I have an ever-growing quilt book collection, many of which have been sourced from thrift stores, that I turn to often for inspiration.

9-PATCH

4-PATCH

BROKEN DISHES

PIN WHEEL

RAIL FENCE

RIBBON STAR

FRIENDSHIP STAR

VARIABLE STAR

OHIO STAR

LEMOYNE STAR

SHOOFLY

DUTCHMAN'S PUZZLE

KING'S CROWN

MAPLE LEAF

LADY OF THE LAKE

SINGLE IRISH CHAIN

HENS & CHICKS

SNOWBALL

SAWTOOTH STAR

BEAR'S PAW

OLD MAID'S PUZZLE

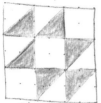

OLD MAID'S PUZZLE

4-PATCH HOURGLASS

CATS CRADLE VARIATION

TOAD IN THE PUDDLE

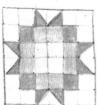

MAPLE STAR

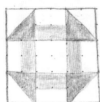

CHURN DASH

BIRDS IN THE AIR

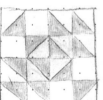

FLYING DUTCHMAN

FLYING GEESE BLOCKS

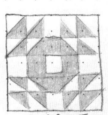

SINGLE WEDDING RING or (crown of Thorns)

LOG CABIN

Jacob's Ladder

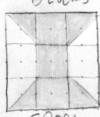

SPOOL

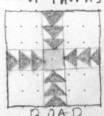

ROAD to CALIFORNIA

AMISH STAR

DOUBLE PINWHEEL

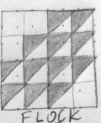

FLOCK OF GEESE

UNION SQUARE

SISTER'S CHOICE

Quilt block sketches

FOUR-PATCH BLOCK TUTORIAL

The first foundational shape I want to introduce is the square, or in this case four squares sewn together to become a four-patch block. A four-patch is usually made from contrasting colors that are alternated. Make a bunch of four-patch blocks and audition different ways of laying out the design before committing to sewing the blocks together. Four-patch blocks set on point (page 157) with spacers are a pretty fun option.

To make the four-patch block, first decide on the size you want each finished block to be. Divide that by two and then add ½ inch (12 mm) for seam allowance. For example, if I want to make 4-inch (10 cm) finished four-patches, then I need to cut 2½-inch (5 cm) squares. Another common and traditional block, the nine-patch, is created the same way, alternating light and dark colors in three rows of three squares.

1. Arrange the squares as shown.

2. Sew the squares together to make two pairs. Press the seams open.

3. With the patchwork facing right sides together, align the seams and pin the pieces together (see page 142).

4. Sew the rows together and press the seam open. Voilà! A four-patch block.

HST TUTORIAL

Half-square triangles are perhaps the most common shape used within quilt blocks. There's hardly a quilt I make that doesn't involve them. There are infinite ways to put them together to form modern geometric shapes, traditional stars, or spiky sawtooth borders. These instructions are for making two at a time. HST construction begins by pairing two (usually) contrasting-colored squares.

When making hundreds of HSTs, it's helpful to come up with some kind of logical production system to speed things up.

To determine what size squares to begin with, we use a formula:

HST formula:
- Finished HST size + 1 inch (2.5 cm)

1. Cut 2 contrasting-colored squares 1 inch bigger than your desired finished HST size.

2. Place the lighter square on top of the darker one, matching all corners. Center the middle line of a ¼-inch (6 mm) seam ruler on opposing corners. With a mechanical pencil, draw a line on both sides of the ruler.

3. Sew along both pencil lines.

4. Cut between the sewn lines, either with scissors or a rotary cutter and ruler.

5. Press the seams open.

6. Place the 45-degree diagonal line of a square quilter's ruler directly over the diagonal seam.

7. Trim a scant bit off the right and top edge. Then rotate the HST and trim the HST to its unfinished size. Trimming HSTs is tedious work, but if you don't trim them, your quilt will likely be wonky and, in extreme cases, may not lie flat. Cue up a podcast, audiobook, or some good tunes and get to trimming.

8. Voilà! Two HSTs.

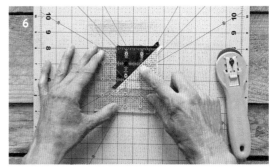

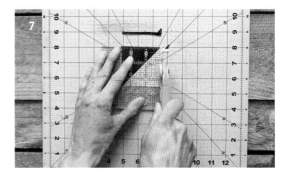

QST TUTORIAL

The quarter-square triangle, also referred to as the hourglass block, is another versatile shape commonly found within traditional quilt blocks. Of course there's a handy formula to determine what size squares to begin with:

QST formula:
- finished block size plus 1½ inches (4 cm)

1. Follow the HST tutorial to make a pair of HSTs, but do not trim them.

2. With right sides facing, place one HST on top of the other with colors opposing and the corners and diagonal seams aligned.

3. Center the middle line of a ¼-inch (6 mm) seam ruler on opposing corners. With a mechanical pencil, draw a line on both sides of the ruler.

4. Sew along both pencil lines.

5. Cut between the lines, either with scissors or a rotary cutter and ruler.

6. Press the seams open. Refer to the HST tutorial to properly trim the QSTs to their unfinished size. Voilà! Two QSTs.

A quilt made exclusively of flying geese

The QST is one of my favorite pieces to work with. Sometimes I make stacks of them and make quilts exclusively of QSTs. Such a quilt looks complicated, but QSTs are quite simple to make. This method of making them makes two at a time.

FLYING GOOSE BLOCK

The flying goose can indeed be made with two HSTs, and sometimes that's a good option, but it's helpful to understand how to make it as a stand-alone shape as well. There are some gorgeous antique and modern quilts made exclusively of flying geese. Flying geese also can be used to make fantastic quilt borders. I prefer to make my geese a bit oversized so I have a little wiggle room when trimming them to their unfinished size. This method makes four geese at a time.

Flying geese formula:
- Geese: Finished flying goose width + 1½ inches (4 cm): cut 1

- Corners: Finished flying goose height + 1¼ inches (4 cm): cut 4
- The width measurement of a flying goose block is always twice the height measurement. The large square is the triangular flying goose shape, and the small squares are the corner triangles that the goose is set into.

1. Set of squares ready to become flying geese

2. Cut the large square from corner to corner and then again from opposite corner to corner to make four triangles.

3. Cut each small square from corner to corner once.

4. The triangles are ready to become geese.

5. Arrange the pieces as shown.

6. Place a corner triangle on top of the goose triangle with right sides together. Pin it in place and sew the pieces together. Press the seam open.

7. Repeat for the other corner triangle.

8. Press the seam open.

9. Trim the top edge leaving ¼ inch (6 mm) above the tip of the goose triangle.

10. Trim the bottom edge to your block's unfinished height.

11. Trim even amounts off the sides of the geese to your unfinished block width.

12. Voilà! Four flying geese.

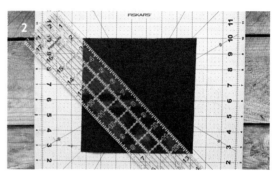

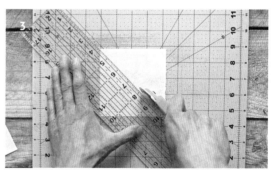

SNOWBALL BLOCK

The snowball block is not a common shape found within traditional quilt blocks, but it is a versatile standalone block, and there are all kinds of different ways to use it in a quilt design. I love to use snowball blocks as spacers because they create a round-looking design from simple squares. The corners can be as deep or narrow as you please. To make a snowball block, cut a square to your desired unfinished block size. Then cut four smaller squares in a contrasting color for the corners. The size of the corner squares depends on how deep you want your corners to be. In this example the unfinished block size is 3½ inches (9 cm) and the corner squares are 1½ inches (4 cm). Have fun experimenting with different-size corner squares.

1. Cut one large square to your unfinished block size. Cut four smaller contrasting-colored squares—their size will depend on how deep you want the corners to be (larger squares for deeper corners). Mark each small square with a diagonal pencil line.

2. Pin a smaller square to each corner with the diagonal lines oriented as shown.

3. Sew along the pencil lines.

4. Trim the seam allowance to ¼ inch (6 mm).

5. Open out the block and press the seams open.

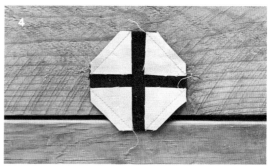

USING A DESIGN WALL AND PLANNING YOUR QUILT LAYOUT

The floor is a fine place to lay out a quilt design, but if you have the wall space, a design wall is an amazing tool. The ability to step back from a design and view it in vertical format is really helpful. It lends an opportunity to move blocks around until the colors are evenly distributed and to audition the blocks as straight set or on-point. You can audition the blocks with spacers or without, and with borders etc., to see how they change the look and feel. Taking photos of the different design layouts as you go is very helpful, because you can see your design from a reduced perspective and look back at the photos to help you make your final design decision.

There are different ways to make design walls, and I encourage you to research them, but the simplest is to tack a large piece of cotton quilt batting to the wall. Quilt pieces stick to the batting like a felt board. Use pins if the blocks slip off.

Spacer Blocks

Some quilt designs are busy with rows of pieced quilt blocks butted right up to each other. Placing pieced blocks right next to each other often creates a dynamic optical illusion or secondary design that makes the eyes dance around the quilt. On the other hand, alternating pieced blocks with plain spacer blocks creates negative space in the design. Negative space highlights the blocks as individuals, giving them the appearance that they're floating rather than melting into each other.

Block Settings

Once all the quilt blocks have been made, they must be joined together to become a quilt top. The typical way to do this is to sew them into horizontal rows and then sew the rows together— this is called a "straight" setting. Another option, which offers visual interest to certain designs, is to rotate the blocks so that their points are up and down, which requires sewing the blocks into diagonal rows; this is called an "on-point" setting.

Straight Setting

1. Arrange the blocks on the floor or design wall into horizontal rows.

2. Sew the blocks into horizontal rows, matching the seams if applicable. Press the seams open.

3. Sew the rows together, matching the seams. Press seams open.

On-Point Setting

Since the diagonal measurement of a square is larger than its measurement from side to side, a block set on point takes up more space in a quilt than a straight-set block. To calculate the diagonal measurement of a block, multiply the length of one finished block's side by 1.414. This will tell you how much space each block will take up horizontally and vertically so you can determine what size blocks to make and how many.

Once all your blocks are made, lay them out on the design wall or floor in diagonal rows. This leaves triangle-shaped gaps along the perimeter of the quilt and at the corners, so additional triangle-shaped pieces are cut to fill the gaps. The triangles in the corners are called corner triangles, and the ones along the perimeter are referred to as side-setting triangles. To determine what size squares to cut, we use a formula:

Corner Triangle Formula
- (Finished block size divided ÷ 1.414) + 1 inch (2.5 cm)
- Round up to the nearest ⅛ inch (3 mm)
- Each square will yield 2 triangles, so you will need to cut 2 squares for the 4 quilt corners.

Side-Setting Triangle Formula
- (Finished block size × 1.414) + 1¼ inches (3 cm)
- Round up to the nearest ⅛ inch (3 mm). Each square yields 4 side-setting triangles.

Let's use the patchwork quilt shown here as an example of the side-setting formula. The finished block size is 2 inches (5 cm).

- $2 \times 1.414 = 2.828 + 1¼ = 4.078$; round up to 4⅛ inches (10.5 cm).

I need to cut 4⅛-inch (10.5 cm) squares for the side-setting triangles, and each square will yield 4 triangles.

To figure out how many side-setting triangles your quilt needs, you can either sketch it out on paper or lay your blocks out on point either on the floor or design wall. Then count the triangular gaps around the perimeter of the quilt and divide that number by 4 to determine how many squares you need to cut. Once the required squares are determined and cut, each square is cross-cut from corner to corner diagonally and then again from opposing corners to yield 4 side-setting triangles. Then determine the size squares required for the corner triangles and cut 2. The corner squares are cut on the diagonal only once.

1. Arrange the blocks in an on-point setting with the side-setting triangles placed along the perimeter and the corner triangles placed in the four corners.

2. Sew the blocks together into diagonal rows.

3. Sew a side triangle to the beginning and end of the diagonal rows.

4. Sew the rows together beginning in the middle (4a), matching the seams as you go, and working your way out to the shorter rows so that the quilt top is in two halves (4b).

5. Sew each half together.

6. Sew the corner triangles in place to complete the quilt top.

7. Press the quilt top gently.

Borders

Great quilt borders can be made from the three shape tutorials I've shared. To avoid having to calculate border math, you can make border pieces whatever size the pieces within the quilt blocks are. For example, let's say I want to put a sawtooth (HST) border on a Variable Star quilt and let's say the star blocks are made from 3-inch (7.5 cm) finished QSTs. I could simply make 3-inch (7.5 cm) finished HSTs for my border and they would fit perfectly with my squares

Sometimes it's necessary to add an unpieced border to a quilt top to size it up a bit or to frame it. This requires careful measuring to keep the quilt top from puckering, which would prevent it from lying flat. The vertical borders are sewn on first and then the horizontal ones. To determine the vertical border length, the quilt top is measured in three places to find the average vertical measurement. To do this, measure from the top right corner to the bottom right corner, then from the top middle edge to the bottom middle edge, then from the top left corner to the bottom left corner. Add those three measurements together and divide by three. That's the length you'll need to cut both vertical borders. To make the border strips, cut your fabric (from selvedge to selvedge) the width of your desired border plus ½ inch (12 mm) for seam allowance. Then sew the strips together end to end. Cut two border strips the length of your average vertical border measurement. Fold the quilt top and the border strip in half and make a crease, then fold in half again to mark the quarter points and make creases there, too. With right sides together, pin the border to the quilt top at the creases. Repeat to make the horizontal borders.

MAKING A CREATIVE QUILT BACK

I most often make pieced quilt backs from whatever I have around that fits the vibe of the front of the quilt. Sometimes I keep them more minimal and other times I use it as an opportunity to "clean out the refrigerator," so to speak, and use up many fabric remnants. Don't be afraid to use imperfect, unevenly dyed fabrics on quilt backs, as they often look surprisingly good there. If you want to make your quilt back the traditional way from one piece, fabric manufacturers sell wide backing fabric, and there are some organic options available.

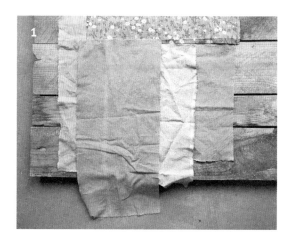

1. Select fabrics for the quilt back. Lay the quilt top on the floor, then begin laying backing fabric pieces over it until it's entirely covered. The back needs to exceed the top by at least 2 inches (5 cm) on all sides so you have wiggle room when hand quilting.

2. Trim up the fabrics so that they can be sewn together. Piecing a quilt back is like a puzzle. You have to study the pieces and figure out a logical order in which it will work to sew them all together.

3. Go with the flow, and don't be afraid to add more fabrics or take some away. When you are happy with the back, the next step is to make a quilt sandwich, page 164.

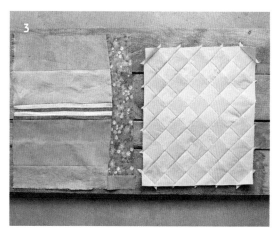

Examples of backs of quilts

Top: Back of the patchwork squares quilt
(page 89)
Bottom: Back of the buffalo check version
(page 93)

Opposite top left: Back of the tumbleweed quilt
(page 95)
Opposite bottom left: Back of an ode to summer quilt
(page 101)
Opposite top right: Back of the jackrabbit quilt
(page 107)
Opposite bottom right: Back of the mycelium quilt
(page 111)

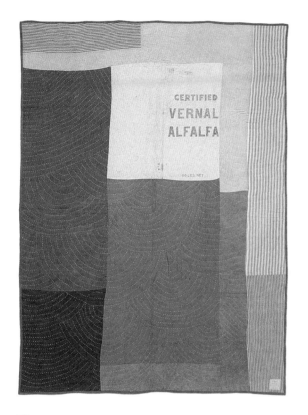

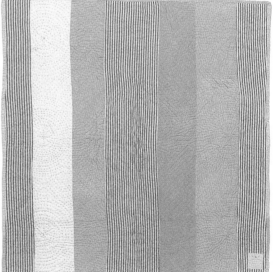

MAKING THE QUILT SANDWICH

A quilt has three layers, consisting of the quilt back, the batting, and the quilt top. A "quilt sandwich" is the first step in uniting the three layers. My favorite types of batting are organic cotton and wool.

1. With the wrong side of the quilt back facing up, tape it to a hard surface with masking or painter's tape, pulling it taut but not overly taut. Cut a piece of batting the same size as the backing and spread it over the backing, smoothing out all the wrinkles, working from the center to the edges.

2. Center the quilt top with the right side facing up on top of the batting and smooth out all the wrinkles. If you wish to mark hand-quilting lines, do so now with a marking tool such as a hera marker, chalk pencil, or water-soluble fabric marker. See the tiny quilt project on page 123 for some hand-quilting ideas.

3. Use large safety pins to baste the layers together, spacing the pins roughly 4 to 6 inches (10 to 15 cm) apart.

Marking straight quilting lines with a hera marker and quilter's ruler

QUILTING OR TYING THE QUILT

The difference between a quilt and a blanket is the layers. They need to be held together, either with quilting stitches or with small ties. The quilting stitches can be done with a machine or by hand. I never dreamed I would have the patience to hand quilt, but when I began making quilts from fabrics I naturally dyed, machine quilting them didn't feel like the right fit. I gave hand quilting a try and fell in love—not only with the process but with the beautiful texture that can be achieved only by human hands. Hand quilting or tying can be done holding the quilt in your lap, or you can use a quilting hoop or frame. I use a frame when I'm quilting straight lines and also for tied quilts, but hold the quilt in my lap when I'm quilting curvy lines, so I can turn the quilt to follow the curves. A frame is nice because it gives the quilt a place while you're working on it, and it can help keep the layers organized, but quilting in your lap is totally great too.

Hand Quilting

There are many different styles of hand stitching and threads to choose from, and they all affect the quilt's texture and aesthetic. The denser the stitches and rows of stitches, the more stiff and rigid the quilt will be. Curvy lines spaced a couple of inches apart will yield a lofty, puffy texture. Try out different styles to see which you prefer, and don't feel like you have to commit to just one. Study quilts you love or photos of quilts you love to see how the maker achieved a certain texture. Once you've tried different methods, think of a way you can uniquely express yourself through hand stitches. With big quilts it's best to begin quilting in the center and work your way out toward the edges. With smaller quilts it's okay to work from edge to edge, but always go in the same direction if you're quilting straight lines.

I like a variety of threads and am not loyal to any one brand. They're all a little different in thickness and feeling. Try sashiko thread, perle cotton, and traditional hand-quilting thread to discover which you prefer. Sashiko thread can be dyed exactly as you would dye a fabric—just be sure to purchase a PFD type that has not been treated to resist dye. Sashiko needles or embroidery needles work well, and you'll need a thimble and a pair of snips. My thimble is a special little thing I found at an antiques store; it's made from sterling silver with little flowers etched on it. I like to imagine the women who used it before me and all the things they made by hand with it.

1. Thread a needle and hold it in your right hand. With your left hand place the tail end of the thread over your needle, leaving about a 1-inch (2.5 cm) tail.

2. Pinch the thread and needle with your right hand to keep the tail in place and wrap the thread around the needle in a counterclockwise motion with your left hand—go around 1 to 2 times with sashiko thread and 4 to 8 times with hand-quilting thread. You'll need to experiment with how many wraps you need depending on your thread and fabric (see step 5).

3. Pinch the wraps with your left forefinger and thumb and pull the needle up with your right hand. Pull until you reach the end of the

thread so the knot rests just before the end of the thread. That's a quilter's knot!

4. Beginning about 1 inch (2.5 cm) from where you wish to begin stitching, push the needle between the quilt top and back layers and pull it through to where you wish to begin stitching.

5. Pop the knot through the top layer into the batting layer. If your knot is too thick, it won't pop through, and if it's too thin it will pull right out. You have to get it just right. If your knot is too big or small, snip it off and make a new one with more or less thread wraps.

6. Begin stitching. Push the needle straight down through all three layers. Poke it through only a tiny bit onto the back side and then rock it back up to the front side. With hand quilting you do not pull the needle all the way to the back and then back up through the top or the stitches on the backside will be crooked. The needle goes down and back up in one motion. Once you get good at "rocking the needle," try taking 3 or 4 stitches at a time to speed things up. When your thread gets low, make a quilter's knot about one stitch length from where you left off and pop the knot between the quilt top and batting. Tug it to bury it well in the batting layer so it won't come loose.

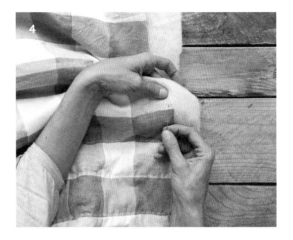

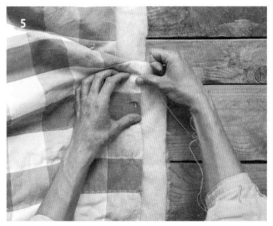

Hand Tying a Quilt

Hand ties, depending on how densely you place them, often preserve the loftiness of the batting, which can make for the warmest, coziest quilts. My grandma made a lot of hand-tied quilts, and it was those quilts my children loved to snuggle up in the most. Sometimes hand tying is quicker than hand quilting, but that depends on the density of the hand-ties. If the ties are spaced very close together they will take much longer than hand stitches. You can use perle cotton, sashiko thread, yarn, or anything of that sort. Sometimes I like to combine hand-quilting stitches with hand ties, as shown here.

Thread a needle with a long piece of yarn or string. Pull the needle from the top of the quilt to the back and come back up about ⅛ inch (3 mm) away. Cut the yarn, leaving tails long enough to easily tie a knot. Tie a box knot, going right over left twice, then left over right twice. For thicker yarns, tie single knots. Trim the ties to your desired length.

BINDING THE QUILT

It's always an exciting feeling to reach the point of binding a quilt, because once the raw edges are bound the quilt is finished! I prefer a double fold binding, which means that the binding fabric is two layers thick for extra durability. Miters look really nice on quilts with square corners, but sometimes it's fun to make a quilt with rounded corners, so I've included a tutorial for that as well.

Double-Fold Mitered Corner Binding

This is my go-to method of binding a quilt with a double layer of fabric for durability and tidy mitered corners.

1. Once the hand quilting is complete, line up the edge of a quilter's ruler with the raw edge of your quilt top and use a rotary cutter to trim off the excess batting and backing so that it's flush with the quilt top.

2. Cut binding strips: I prefer to cut my binding strips from selvedge to selvedge rather than the traditional way of cutting them on the bias. Although unorthodox, this method makes it easier to calculate the math, wastes less fabric, and, most importantly, totally works. To determine the total length of binding fabric you need, add 20 inches (50 cm) to your quilt perimeter. To determine how many strips of your fabric cut selvedge to selvedge you'll need, divide your binding length by the width of your binding fabric. As an example, my tiny quilt perimeter is 60 inches (152 cm). Total binding needed: 60 + 20 = 80 inches (202 cm). The width of my binding fabric is 20 inches

(50 cm), and 80 divided by 20 = 4. So I need to cut 4 binding strips. Round up if your strip amount is uneven.

I cut my binding strips 2¾ inches (7 cm) wide.

3. To make the strips into one piece of continuous binding, lay one strip on top of another, perpendicular, with right sides facing as shown. Draw a diagonal line from corner to corner and sew along the line. Repeat until all your strips are joined.

4. Trim the seam allowance to ¼ inch (6 mm) and press the seams open.

5. Fold the strip in half lengthwise so the raw edges are aligned and press.

6. With the quilt top face up, align the raw edges of the quilt and binding. Leave a tail of about 8 inches (20 cm) unsewn at the beginning. Sew the binding to the quilt with a ¼ inch (6 mm) seam allowance, beginning where indicated in the photo. Stop sewing ¼ inch (6 mm) before you reach the corner, and backstitch a few stitches.

7. To make a mitered corner, fold the binding up at a 45 degree angle and press.

8. Fold the binding back down over itself, aligning the raw edges, and press again. Begin sewing right at the edge. Sew to the next corner and repeat the mitering process.

9. Stop sewing when you get about 8 inches (20 cm) from where you began.

10. Overlap the two ends of the binding so that they overlap by 2¾ inches (7 cm), trimming away excess binding from both ends.

11. Unfold both binding ends. With right sides facing, place the top strip perpendicular to the bottom strip as shown. Draw a diagonal line and pin the pieces to hold them in place. Stitch the binding only along the line, trim the seam to ¼ inch (6 mm), and press it open. Refold the binding in half and press.

12. Sew the remaining binding in place.

13. Turn the quilt over to the backside and fold the binding over the raw edge, pressing and pinning it in place as you go so that it covers the seam line. Fold the corners to form miters. Hand-sew the binding in place with a whip stitch.

Rounded Corner Binding

Although mitered corners are really simple to make, sometimes it's fun to make a quilt with soft, rounded corners. To create this style of binding, simply use a round object and a marking tool to round the corners as shown in step 10 of the Broken Dishes Quilt Poncho pattern (page 117). Follow the Double-Fold Mitered Corner Binding instruction on page 168, but when you come to a round corner, ease the binding around the gentle curve instead of folding a mitered corner.

CARING FOR YOUR QUILTS

After all the beautiful work you've invested in making a quilt, it's important to take good care of all that amazingness. If a quilt is not visibly dirty, you can bring it outdoors and hang it on the clothesline for some fresh air. Sometimes, though, your quilts will need a good wash.

To wash a quilt, fill a bathtub about halfway with cold to lukewarm water. Add a small amount of pH-neutral natural liquid detergent to the water and swish it around really well before adding the quilt. Let the quilt soak for a few minutes and agitate it. If there's a stain, rub it with your hands, but never put soap or detergent directly on a naturally dyed fabric. I learned this the hard way a couple times—once with soap flakes that didn't dissolve all the way and made permanent white spots all over some fabric I dyed, and another time I poured a natural powdered laundry detergent on a stain and it totally stripped the fabric of dye in every area that the detergent touched. Harsh!

After the quilt has soaked a bit in the bathtub, drain the water and then fill the tub again with enough water to rinse the soap away. It's best

to have another person with you to help gently squeeze as much water as you can out of the quilt. At this point it can be taken outside to hang on the line or put in the washing machine on a spin cycle before hanging. If you have a front-loading washing machine you can wash quilts on a gentle cycle, but the washing machine is harder on a quilt than hand washing.

As the years go on your quilt will eventually need some mending, and there are all kinds of wonderful mending books and resources available to help you with that.

resources

Some of my favorite artists, farms, and natural dye and fiber stockists to support. Many offer classes and workshops that I highly recommend!

Aboubakar Fofana
aboubakarfofana.com

Botanical Colors
botanicalcolors.com

Dixza
dixza.com

The Dogwood Dyer
thedogwooddyer.com

Farm & Folk
Farmandfolk.com

Fedco
fedcoseeds.com

Grand Prismatic Seed
grandprismaticseed.com

Porfirio Gutiérrez
porfiriogutierrez.com

Hemp Traders
hemptraders.com

Life-Giving Linen
lifegivinglinen.com

Maiwa
maiwa.com

Organic Cotton Plus
organiccottonplus.com

Shibori Dragon
shiboridragon.com

Stony Creek Colors
stonycreekcolors.com

Tarai Blue
indigodesign.in

Winona's Hemp Heritage Farm
winonashemp.com

YLI
ylicorp.com

acknowledgments

It's surreal to be at the end of this book-writing journey. A whole year of work, and then some, is encapsulated in these pages. It took the help and encouragement of many talented people, all of whom I'm grateful for. Thank you first to Meredith Clark, who approached me one early spring day and offered me the opportunity to write this book. Your timing was divine, and I'm so glad I took the giant leap of faith to say yes.

The photography for this book was a wonderful collaboration. Thank you to my incredibly talented friend Chandler Strange and to my daughter, Ila, for being willing to drop what you were doing and run outside with me when the light was "just perfect." The images you both created are perfectly authentic and such a valuable contribution to this book. Scott Smith contributed the wonderful flat-lay quilt photographs, and to him I am also grateful.

Thank you to my editor, Shawna Mullen, and the team at Abrams for your expertise in putting this book together so beautifully. Thank you to designer Darilyn Carnes for all your hard work and for making this book feel so authentic to me.

I'm grateful to the matrons of my family, Nancy, Millie, and Flo. Their hands were always busy making something beautiful, and it's an honor to carry on their traditions. Thank you also to my dad, David, who so patiently let me participate in his woodworking projects when I was a child. It turns out it was those seemingly little things that ended up being most profound and formative.

Thank you to all the many friends and folks who have cheered me on and encouraged me and offered support and advice throughout this book-writing process.

Thank you to my children, Isaac, Asher, Yuri, and Ila. All my love and all the seeds I plant are for you, always.

Lastly and most importantly, thank you to my husband, Tom. Our togetherness is integral to this life we've forged as farmers and artists. For that and to you I am grateful.

about the author

Sara is an organic farmer, natural dyer, and textile artist residing in the high desert of Southwest Colorado. *Farm & Folk* is an expression of her work as both farmer and artist. A lifelong student and steward of the land, Sara takes inspiration from the paradigm-shifting, slow processes of tending soil, seeds, and plants. Her experience and direct connection to food, natural color, and fiber have deepened her understanding and appreciation of their value, a connection her naturally dyed quilts embody. See new and current work at farmandfolk.com and at @farmandfolk.

Editor: Shawna Mullen
Designer: Darilyn Lowe Carnes
Managing Editor: Lisa Silverrman
Production Manager: Kathleen Gaffney

Library of Congress Control Number: 2023930554

ISBN: 978-1-4197-6199-7
eISBN: 978-1-64700-676-1

Text copyright © 2023 Sara Larson Buscaglia
Photographs copyright © Sara Larson Buscaglia
Photographs on pp. 11, 105, 132, 133, 160 by Ila Buscaglia;
pp. 19, 41, 46, 61, 62, 65, 172 by Chandler Strange;
pp. 86, 94, 100, 106, 110, 162, 163, and endpapers by Scott Smith

Cover © 2023 Abrams

Printed and bound in China
10 9 8 7 6 5 4 3 2 1

Abrams books are available at special discounts when purchased
in quantity for premiums and promotions as well as fundraising
or educational use. Special editions can also be created to
specification. For details, contact specialsales@abramsbooks.com
or the address below.

ABRAMS The Art of Books
195 Broadway, New York, NY 10007
abramsbooks.com